CLOCKS

THE BRITISH MUSEUM
CLOCKS

David Thompson
Photography by Saul Peckham

THE BRITISH MUSEUM PRESS

For Pam, who always finds time.

First published in 2004 by The British Museum Press
A division of The British Museum Company Ltd
46 Bloomsbury Street, London WC1B 3QQ

David Thompson has asserted the right to be identified
as the author of this work

A catalogue record for this book is available from the
British Library

ISBN 0–7141–2812–0

Designed and typeset in Scala by Andrew Shoolbred
Printed in Barcelona by Grafos S.A.

FRONTISPIECE: Movement of a longcase clock by
Ahaseurus Fromanteel (pp. 74–5).

OPPOSITE: Detail of milkmaid automaton (see pp. 34–5).

Page 7: Detail of travelling clock by Thomas Mudge (see pp. 120–1).

Contents

The pendulum clock and the age of London supremacy

Eighteenth-century opulence

Precision timekeeping in the eighteenth century

Acknowledgements

This book, which is my first, and indeed the first on the clocks in The British Museum since Hugh Tait's *Clocks & Watches* in 1984, has been made possible thanks to the kindness and generous support of Mr Simon Hogg. My thanks go to Simon for suggesting the project to me in the first place and for his help in putting a book on the wonderful clocks in the British Museum back on the bookshelves for everyone to enjoy.

I owe a great debt to my British Museum colleagues Jeremy Evans and Paul Buck, whose support has been invaluable. My thanks to Jeremy for his never-ending generosity in passing on so much information and for his ability to save me from many a 'you-clod-you' statement, to which I am particularly prone. I am also grateful to Paul who has supplied a seemingly constant stream of clocks to the photographic studios and also for giving me much useful information regarding the clocks which I chose to include. I am also grateful to my former boss, John Leopold who, as always, has been generous to a fault with his encyclopaedic knowledge of horological history and technology.

While some of the photographs in this book are the work of former colleagues in the museum's Photographic Department the vast majority of pictures were taken by Saul Peckham, who I am sure everyone will agree, has done a superb job of bringing to life the many and varied clocks which appear in this volume. Anyone who has tried to take photographs of clocks will realise just how difficult it is to get good results. Saul shows us here what can be achieved through skill and tenacity, even when yet another 'absolutely necessary' picture was asked for, long past the final date for completion of the project.

Just round the corner at The British Museum Press were the editor Charlie Mounter and the picture researcher Beatriz Waters. Charlie approached the task of keeping me on the straight and narrow, making sure I kept within my word limits and dealing with my excesses, with admirably patient professionalism. She also has a lightness of spirit which made the otherwise tedious task of correcting proofs a much more pleasant job. It is thanks to her that this book is not two hundred pages over-size and riddled with my shortcomings. The pictures were organised by Beatriz, who made sure that all the relevant materials were obtained and delivered to Andrew Shoolbred. Andrew has designed a book which to my mind is of elegant appearance and at the same time shows the clocks to their best advantage.

Lastly I thank my wife Pam for her excellent and frighteningly rapid translation of *L'Horloge Amoureuse*. Much more than that, I thank her for reading and correcting my numerous versions of texts. But more than anything else, I thank her for all the years of support and encouragement. It was Pam who said in 1977 – 'why don't you go to Hackney College and learn this clock and watch business properly? If I can get a decent job in London you could do the two-year course and start a new career that you would enjoy'. I must say that all that time ago, I never dreamt that it would lead to this.

L'Horloge Amoureuse

L'Orloge est,
Au vray considerer,
Une instrument tres bel et tres notable,
Est s'est aussy plaisant et pourfitable,
Car nuict et iours les heures nous aprent
Par la soubtilite qu'elle comprent
En l'absence meisme dou soleil:
Dont on doit mieuls prisier son appareil,
Ce que les autre instruments ne font pas,
Tant soient faits part art et par compas:
Dont celi tiens pour vaillant et pour sage
Qui en treuva primierement l'usage
Quant par son sens il commenca et fit
Chose si noble et de si grant proufit . . .

Jean Froissart, 1369

The Clock, forsooth,
Considered in all truth
An instrument of beauty and repute,
And also it is pleasing and of use,
For night and day the hours it doth proclaim
By all the subtlety its works contain
Even when the sun cannot be seen:
And thus one should so value one's machine
As other instruments cannot so perform
Howe'er by art and accuracy informed:
And so we judge him valiant and wise
Who first discovery made of this device
And by his knowledge, started and devised
A thing so noble and so greatly prized . . .

Translation by Pamela Thompson, 2004

Introduction

The British Museum is home to one of the finest collections of clocks and watches in the world. With a public exhibition showing the development of mechanical horology over the centuries and a dedicated Students' Room available to those who wish to study the subject of horology in greater depth, The British Museum is unique. With more than a thousand clocks and 4,500 watches, the history of horology is perhaps covered in greater depth and diversity than in any other collection. This history, from medieval times to the highly organised industrial societies of the modern world, is a diverse and fascinating one. It encompasses a multitude of disciplines, providing insights into the history of science, the development of decorative arts, social history through the people who owned and used the clocks, and perhaps most importantly an understanding of the development of the art, science and industry of the clockmaker.

The work of these craftsmen can most logically be looked at from three different perspectives. The first is from the point of view of the men whose fundamental objective was the supply of ever more accurate machines to meet the demands of scientists, navigators and astronomers. Secondly, there were those who saw their future in the making of the most lavish and beguiling luxury goods for a clientele for whom money was no object. And lastly, there were those clock- and watchmakers who strove to make their merchandise cheaper than their competitors in order to reach a wider market. In many instances, these men were simply retailers, who might well have been trained as clock- or watch makers but who used their skills in the retailing, repairing and maintaining of clocks and watches. The British Museum is rich in examples of the fruits of all these labours, which range from the most prized pieces of the clockmakers' art to mass-produced, cheap and shoddy goods which provide a startling contrast to some of the finest examples of precision horology ever to have been made. No collection could possibly be all-encompassing and indeed no book, short of a twenty-five-volume catalogue, could reveal all the secrets of a collection, but here it is hoped that some of the fascinating clocks held in The British Museum will be revealed in their detailed finery or humble simplicity. It is also hoped that some idea of the range and diversity of clocks over the centuries will be demonstrated and that this introductory glimpse into the world of horology will encourage the reader to look further into this most absorbing of subjects.

TOP RIGHT: Montagu House, an engraving by Sutton Nicholls, c.1714.

BOTTOM RIGHT: The British Museum as it looks today, showing part of the south front and courtyard.

The Origins and Purpose
of Clocks

That science has to some extent always been dependent on the progress of horology has been largely overlooked. Everyone knows the names of great scientists such as Galileo Galilei, Isaac Newton and Albert Einstein, but how many are familiar with those of Christiaan Huygens and Robert Hooke, or the clockmakers Thomas Tompion, George Graham, Thomas Mudge, Abraham Louis Breguet and John Harrison, let alone Essen and Parry, who made the first atomic clock in 1955?

To this day, the origins of the mechanical clock remain obscure. The new machines which appeared towards the end of the thirteenth century were preceded by sundials and water clocks. It has been suggested that the mechanical clock might have derived from the monumental planetary models powered by water which existed in earlier centuries in China, the Middle East and north Africa. Whatever their origins, the first records of mechanical clocks appear towards the end of the thirteenth century in the form of manuscript references to new installations in England and in northern Italy. It should be noted, however, that this is where records have survived and not necessarily where the first clocks were made.

In 1271 Robert the Englishman, in his commentary on Johannes de Sacrobosco's *Tractus de Sphera Mundi*, states that clockmakers had not by then found a way to make a wheel rotate once per equinoctial cycle. In about 1275 Albrecht, the author of *Juengeren Titurel*, describes a clock showing the passage of the sun, moon and planets. One of the earliest references to an actual clock exists in the archives of Exeter Cathedral, where there is an account of repairs made to the bells, musical instruments and the clock. One of the more intriguing references exists in the archives of St Paul's Cathedral, London, where the brewer's account for 1286 shows that Bartholomo Orologario (Bartholomew the clockmaker) was given twenty-three bowls of beer, although it does not say over what period.

By the fourteenth century large public clocks were relatively common in Europe and by the middle of the following century the smaller domestic clock had appeared. These domestic clocks ranged from items of status in the medieval and Renaissance periods, to clocks intended to furnish fine houses in the seventeenth and eighteenth centuries and to mass-produced clocks for all in the nineteenth and twentieth centuries.

Throughout the centuries clocks were also intrinsically bound to scientific understanding and advancement in which time measurement was central. Astronomers and navigators had need of the most accurate timekeepers available and constantly demanded better. At all times, however, accuracy and precision were relative terms. The precision of the finest pendulum clock made by Thomas Tompion for the Greenwich Royal Observatory in 1676 was perceived as the height of accuracy, just as today we regard the atomic time standard.

At the same time, in the sixteenth and seventeenth centuries the princely *Kunstkammer*, or art cabinet, was the place where elaborate and complex clocks could be found within the learned owners' scientific collections. Such clocks represented the latest and most impressive items of technological and decorative achievement, intended to both educate and astound.

While no examples from the earliest period of clockmaking exist in the Museum's collections, developments from 1450 onwards are well represented. Clocks from the sixteenth and seventeenth centuries reflect an age when they were as much items of status and demonstrations of wealth as they were machines used to measure time and regulate everyday life. In this context, it has to be remembered that those people who were wealthy enough to afford a clock (in the main, members of the royal and aristocratic families of Europe) did not live their lives in the shadow of time, as we do today. For this reason clocks from the fifteenth to the mid-seventeenth century must be looked at in the context of their age. The ownership of a clock which showed the time, struck the hours and the quarters and was furnished with an alarm, such as the anonymous Gothic wall clock (pp. 22–3) must be seen as a measure of the owner's wealth. Clocks made before the introduction of the pendulum in 1657 would have been incapable of keeping time to anything better than a quarter of an hour per day, and their performance would have been erratic.

The application of the pendulum to clocks by Christiaan Huygens in 1657 and the resulting clocks made under his patent by Salomon Coster in The Hague paved the way for a new era in clockmaking, in which the clock took on a role for its owner as an instrument of time measurement as well as a luxury item. The introduction of the pendulum led to a different kudos for the clock. Accuracy improved from about half an hour per day and an erratic performance to one minute or even less per day.

Now the boast would more likely be about accuracy than it would be about luxury. As the centuries progressed, so the number of clockmakers increased dramatically and the price of clocks fell relative to the spending ability of the buyers. During the seventeenth and eighteenth centuries, nearly every small European town had a clockmaker and the ownership of clocks had spread to the merchant classes and rich farmers. During the nineteenth century, the introduction of machine-made clocks and the diverse industry in areas such as the Black Forest in Germany, the Jura in France and Switzerland, and New England in America reduced prices to such an extent that ownership of clocks spread to the common people and the phrase 'a clock for everyman' could be applied throughout Europe and America.

The Collectors and Collections

The history of horology in The British Museum is intrinsically linked with a group of individuals without whose generous support the Museum would not be the great horological centre it is today. It is through the generosity and discernment of these benefactors that the Museum has such a magnificent collection.

SIR AUGUSTUS WOLLASTON FRANKS

The collections of medieval and Renaissance clocks in The British Museum exist largely thanks to two collectors. The first of these is Sir Augustus Wollaston Franks, a record of whose life and career was published in a monograph in 1984 by the then Director of the British Museum, Sir David Wilson. Until then Franks' importance in the history of the Museum had gone largely unnoticed. He was born in 1826 and educated at Eton and Trinity College, Cambridge. Franks came to The British Museum in 1851 and in 1866 was made Keeper of British and Medieval Antiquities and Ethnography. In this role, and as Director of the Society of Antiquaries of London, it was he who encouraged leading collectors of the age to become closely involved with the Museum and its collections. In an unpublished manuscript, written some time between 1888 and 1897 and entitled 'The Apology of My Life by A.W.F.' Franks wrote, 'The medieval and later collections have chiefly grown by gift or bequest . . . The three principal bequests have come from my own personal and intimate friends whom I have helped in forming their collections. These were Mr. Slade, Mr. Henderson and Mr. Octavius Morgan'. Franks himself either gave or bequeathed to the Museum more than 22,000 items, including 103 of a horological nature. In addition to seventy-nine scientific instruments there are thirteen watches, some watch cases and a small number of clocks.

OCTAVIUS MORGAN

Charles Octavius Swinnerton Morgan was one of the great collectors of horology in the nineteenth century. In addition to being the Member of Parliament for Monmouth, Morgan was a Fellow of the Royal Society and of the Royal Archaeological Institute. He was a vice president of the Society of Antiquaries of London and a prominent figure in archaeological and antiquarian circles in South Wales. He was born in 1803, the son of Sir Charles Morgan of Tredegar House, Newport. In later years he lived in Pall Mall in London and at The Friars in Newport, a house which he had extensively renovated in a neo-Tudor style to suit his taste and to complement his collections largely of Renaissance material. In the 1850s Morgan exhibited clocks and watches to assemblies of the London Society of Antiquaries and the Royal Archaeological Institute.

The first official contact which Morgan had with the Museum was in 1853, when he wrote to Augustus Wollaston Franks in an effort to persuade the Trustees to acquire a magnificent carillon clock by Isaac Habrecht of Strasbourg. Unfortunately they were not favourably disposed toward the clock, but Morgan did purchase it for his own collection and took it to The Friars where it stood at the bottom of the main staircase until his death in 1888.

Octavius Morgan again wrote to Franks in 1866 with news of yet another magnificent piece of Renaissance clockwork in the form of a medieval ship, and this time the trustees were pleased to accept Morgan's most generous gift. The following year Morgan presented another fine clock; a magnificent tabernacle clock made in Krakow in 1648, perhaps in memory of the death of King Wladyslaw IV Wasa. Octavius Morgan died in 1888 leaving to the nation his collection of three-hundred items to be housed in the British Museum. In addition to papal rings and chamberlains' keys of office, the horological element of this extraordinary bequest consisted of 239 objects. Of these, the best-known is the carillon clock made in 1589 by Isaac Habrecht (pp. 48–51), as a domestic version of the great astronomical clock he had built for Strasbourg Cathedral. Standing more than five feet high, the clock is an impressive combination of Renaissance decoration and mechanical achievement. In addition to the Habrecht clock, Morgan left to the Museum a diverse and fascinating collection of clocks and watches, particularly from the seventeenth century, amongst them a number of rare examples of the stackfreed watch. His collection of scientific instruments contained a wide variety of sundials, compendia and measuring instruments.

In a tribute to Morgan's life, the President of the Society of Antiquaries of London said:

> His house, the Friars in Newport Monmouthshire was a complete museum, rich in collections of every kind. The most important of these he has most liberally bequeathed to the nation, and those who have examined the watches, clocks and astronomical instruments, the series of papal rings and the chamberlaines' keys now exhibited in the British Museum, may form some idea of the value of this legacy and feel grateful; that collections brought together with such judgement and perseverance were not destined to be dispersed. The great clock now standing at the head of the Principal staircase, and made by the same hands as the celebrated clock of Strasbourg would alone have been a princely donation. Personally Mr Octavius Morgan was a delightful companion, full of information on his favourite subjects, and willing to impart it, and all our fellows of the older generation will ever cherish his memory with respect.

SIR CHARLES FELLOWS

Sir Charles Fellows was a man of many talents. In addition to making the thirteenth recorded ascent of Mont Blanc, he also led a number of expeditions to Asia Minor on behalf of the British Museum, bringing back many important treasures from Lycia.

In 1875 Octavius Morgan published in the *Archaeological Journal* a paper entitled 'Observations on the Classification and Arrangement of a Collection of Watches'. It deals to a large extent with the way in which he viewed his own collection, but it almost certainly derives from a request from his friend, Augustus Wollaston Franks, to assess the Fellows collection, bequeathed to The British Museum in the previous year. In his paper, Morgan says,

> 'I am not aware of anyone besides myself who has made a regular collection of watches, except the late Sir Charles Fellows, and his collection his widow, on her decease last year, munificently bequeathed to The British Museum where they may be seen and much information on the subject gained from them.'

There were in fact more than ninety items in this collection mostly dating from the seventeenth century, and while there were undoubtedly many more watches in the collection than clocks, the small group of clocks is significant.

COURTENAY ADRIAN ILBERT

It is perhaps a fitting coincidence in the history of the Museum's horological collections that the year of Octavius Morgan's death was also the year of Courtenay Ilbert's birth. Ilbert, by profession a civil engineer, became one of the great horological collectors of the twentieth century. He collected widely and over the years built up one of the most comprehensive collections in the world, covering virtually every aspect of the history and development of mechanical horology. When Ilbert's estate was settled in 1958 his vast collection was destined for the London salerooms. There were approximately 2,300 watches and watch movements, forty marine chronometers and 210 clocks, including the famous Drummond Robertson collection of Japanese clocks, and various prints, horological tools, watch papers and other items of horological interest. With the sale catalogue of clocks already printed and the watch catalogue in preparation, it seemed inevitable that the collection would be split up and dispersed around the world.

Following a short but concerted effort by Museum curators of the time and members of the Worshipful Company of Clockmakers under the direction of its Master, M.L. Bateman, an anonymous benefactor emerged (later revealed as Sir Gilbert Edgar CBE, chairman of H. Samuel Watches Ltd), who was prepared to buy the clocks for the nation and put further funds towards the purchase of the rest of Ilbert's collection. His generous offer was accepted and the clocks were saved. With further funds raised by a public subscription organized by the Clockmakers' Company and a hard-won grant from the Treasury to make up the shortfall, Ilbert's collection was saved in its entirety for the British Museum.

Many items from the Ilbert Collection are familiar to horologists around the world. Particularly well-known is the clock by Nicholas Vallin (pp. 56–7) dated 1598, which plays music on thirteen bells at each quarter. Other notable clocks include an early English lantern clock (pp. 62–3) by William Bowyer, with its original balance wheel, the famous 'Mulberry' longcase clock by Thomas Tompion (pp. 90–1) and the fascinating table clock by Thomas Mudge (pp. 118–9), with its very accurate lunar indication and remontoire-driven lever escapement. Examples of the work of continental makers include marine chronometers by Breguet and Berthoud and Breguet's astronomer's follower clock (pp. 136–7).

FRANK H. KNOWLES-BROWN

Frank Knowles-Brown (1897–1965) was a leading figure in the Gemmological Association and in 1953 was a founder member and first chairman of the Antiquarian Horological Society. He had a passion for Gothic clocks and early turret clocks. Following his death, eleven items came to the British Museum. They included a set of medieval striking jacks which Knowles-Brown himself bequeathed. A further four clocks were purchased by Mr and Mrs Gilbert Edgar and presented to the Museum. The remaining six clocks were given by Mrs Clark, Mrs Richard and the Reverend J.H. Knowles-Brown, all beneficiaries of the estate.

LOOKING TO THE FUTURE

Since the arrival of the Ilbert Collection, the Museum has continued to acquire items by purchase and donation. Particularly interesting acquisitions have been the Cassiobury Park turret clock (pp. 60–1) dating from the first half of the seventeenth century, one of a small group of turret clocks marked with a scallop-shell, and a rare English horizontal table clock by Robert Grinkin junior (pp. 64–5), made in about 1650. One of the most impressive of the recent acquisitions has been Thomas Tompion's year-going spring-driven table clock, known as the 'Mostyn' Tompion (pp. 84–7). A prime example of his mechanical pre-eminence, the clock was made for William III in about 1689. A more modern item is the superb carriage clock made by Nicole Nielsen of Soho Square (pp. 160–1) in about 1905 with its superb tourbillon escapement. The most modern clock in the collections is a Junghans radio-time clock tuned to receive time signals transmitted from Rugby and generated by a caesium atomic clock. Such clocks are said to have an accuracy of one second in a million years – a long way removed from Bartholomew drinking his beer whilst tending the St Paul's Cathedral clock in 1286.

Anonymous

Spring-driven chamber clock
Burgundy, mid-fifteenth century
Height 29.5 cm, width 19 cm, depth 17 cm

Documentary references to domestic clocks in the court of Philip the Good, Duke of Burgundy (1419–1467) are supported by the existence of two clocks, both of which are attributed to the middle of the fifteenth century and both of which were spring-driven. One is now in the Germanisches National Museum in Nuremberg and the other, belonging to the Victoria & Albert Museum, has been transferred on indefinite loan to the British Museum. Although this clock has been converted to be weight-driven, there is ample evidence to attest to the fact that it was originally spring-driven. Indeed, to underline the point, Beresford Hutchinson, a former curator of clocks and watches at the Museum, made a reconstruction of the movement to show the original arrangement of the spring barrels and fusees, based on evidence provided by the original clock.

That such clocks existed in Burgundy in the mid-fifteenth century is confirmed by inventories of Philip the Good. In one list, compiled on 12 July 1420, can be found: 'Item: a small square clock, gilt on the outside, and its white enamelled zodiac has one bell on top to ring the hours.' In an inventory of Margaret of Burgundy of 1423 there is 'a small gilt clock. There are two panels on either side made of gilt silver, as is also the dial'. These references do not say whether or not the clocks were weight- or spring-driven but they were both small in size and therefore could well have been spring-driven.

The gothic style is evident here in the upper frieze of roundels, the top of the main outer frame and the quatrefoil decoration in a lozenge pattern around the bottom. Perhaps alluding even more closely to cathedral architecture are the niches in the pillars, each of which contains a standing figure of a saint. To add to the decorative opulence of the clock, the uprights at the top are shaped to form spires rising from the corners of the hexagon, and originally there would have been a further level of similar pillars supporting the bell.

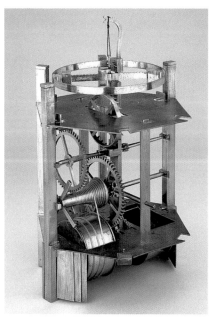

ABOVE: Beresford-Hutchinson's model of the movement.

The movement has hexagonal top and bottom plates with iron bars mounted vertically between them to provide bearings for the gear trains for timekeeping and hour striking. In common with many clocks made in the following century, here the count-wheel and the wheel-work for the dial are placed at right angles to the main gear trains.

Sadly much of the clock is now missing, there is no dial and most of the wheel-work is replaced. There is enough evidence to support the fact that the clock was originally spring-driven with fusees and that the large spring barrels were mounted in the lower part of the movement, as is demonstrated by the modern reconstruction.

Victoria & Albert Museum loan
(Reg. M11–1940)

Anonymous

Weight-driven wall clock with castellated dial
Germany, c.1520
Height 51 cm, width 27.5 cm, depth 3.4 cm

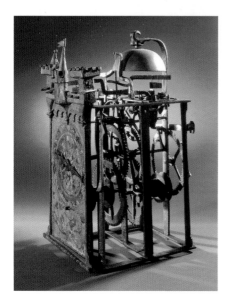

Clocks from the early part of the sixteenth century are relatively rare, but there are a few surviving examples which give us an insight into their appearance and function. This particular clock has undergone some changes over the centuries, some of them quite early in its long history. It was probably made in about 1520 in Germany and shows elements of the Gothic style in the decoration on the corner pillars of the frame.

The gear train for the time keeping is short with only two wheels driving a verge escapement. This escapement keeps the bar-foliot swinging by impulsing it through the pallets, and the rate is controlled by the foliot as it swings back and forth. The period of swing of the foliot can be adjusted by moving the small weights at its outer ends either inwards to make it go faster or outwards to slow it down.

Such clocks as this one were illustrated in the Almanus manuscript, a document written in the 1480's which describes a series of thirty clocks that Brother Paulus Almanus had dealt with and recorded between about 1475 and 1480. As his name suggests, Frater Paulus Almanus was a friar named Paul, of German origin. Nothing much is known of him except that he was living in Rome when he wrote his manuscript and that he handled clocks from a variety of sources. His notes describe both weight- and spring-driven clocks and he concentrates on the description of the complications of the clocks, and their striking mechanisms in particular. A point also worth noting in the manuscript is that all the clocks are constructed on the posted-frame principle in which the bars for the train wheels are held within a four-posted frame. Essentially, this construction derives from turret clockmaking practice.

This clock has, like so many others, been altered from its original construction and may well have started life as a small turret clock intended to drive an external dial. It probably had capstan winding originally. The crown-wheel is a recent replacement made in the Museum.

The dial is not original, but it is likely to be of sixteenth or at least seventeenth century origin, when the clock was turned into a domestic version with its own dial. There are various plugged holes in the plates, suggesting that the clock once had lead-off work to an external dial. In its later guise, however, it would have been mounted on a bracket situated high up the wall in order to give the weights plenty of room to descend and provide a reasonable running time at each wind.

F.H. Knowles Brown Collection
(Reg. 1967,6–1.1)

Anonymous

Gothic wall clock
South Germany, mid-sixteenth century
Height 50 cm, width 15 cm, depth 29 cm

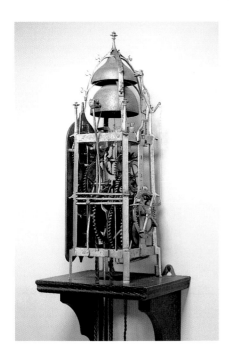

The Gothic style persisted in clock design until very late in the sixteenth century, particularly in the Germanic states and in northern Switzerland. This was, despite the fact that the style was by then old-fashioned, based as it was on the architecture of an earlier period. On this clock, the Gothic style is visible in the buttress corner posts of the frame, decorative elements on the bell straps and the zoomorphic hammer-heads in the form of dragons, each with a ball in its mouth.

This weight-driven clock was designed to stand on a wall bracket and its duration would have depended on how high up the wall it was mounted. Clearly the mechanism would stop when the weights reached the floor. Although the painted-metal dial is a modern replacement it is relatively correct in style. The verge escapement controlled by a weighted foliot is also a modern reconstruction, which probably replaces an anchor escapement with pendulum, added in the seventeenth or eighteenth century to modernize the clock.

There are separate striking trains for the hours and the quarters and for the alarm. The clock also has lunar indications on the dial. Another interesting feature worth noting is that clocks of this period had no friction drive to allow the hand to be set to time independently of the gear train. Instead, to change the time, the owner would lift a small lever fitted at the front of the clock, which when raised lifts the verge out of engagement with the crown wheel, and allows the wheel train to revolve under the control of the adjuster. The lever is then lowered when the hand arrives at the correct time, thus re-engaging the verge with the crown wheel and stopping the wheels from turning rapidly.

The alarm release is performed by a revolving disc on the dial which carries the hour hand. This disc is drilled around the outside with a series of holes in which the pin can be placed according to the desired time for the alarm to sound. As the disc rotates, at the appointed time the pin lifts a lever behind the dial, which in turn releases the alarm mechanism to ring the bell with repeated blows of the hammer.

Ilbert Collection
(Reg. CAI–2136)

Anonymous 'M' or 'W'

Planispheric astrolabic clock
France, c.1560
Height 30.7 cm, base diameter 16.2 cm, vertical dial diameter 11.9 cm

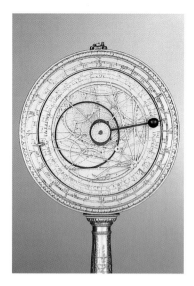

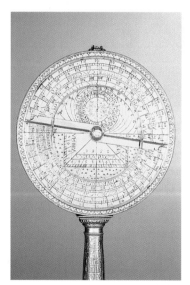

This rare French clock has a clockwork-driven astrolabic dial, with features similar to those on an actual astrolabe. The base houses a large spring-driven iron movement with fusee, verge escapement and balance but the brass balance-bridge and balance are not original. The gilt-brass base has fine engravings of the signs of the zodiac around the side, and its upper surface is engraved with concentric rings showing the Ptolemaic universe. The central column, engraved with the hours of the day and their ruling planets, conceals an arbor which drives the dial.

The planispheric astrolabe is marked for hours around the outside. Within this, a revolving rete with star pointers is engraved with a degree scale and the signs of the zodiac. To the left a steel circle carries a small bead to show the sun's position in the ecliptic. To the right a small moon revolves to show the moon's position in the zodiac and rotates to show its phase. The time is shown by a pointer fixed to the solar plate which revolves once per day. Under the revolving rete is a fixed reversible plate engraved with polar projections to show the positions of the stars. One side is for use at latitude 48° north, and the other side is engraved for latitude 51° 32' north, probably for London. The French inscriptions and the general design suggest that, although unsigned except for a gothic letter 'M' or 'W' on the base, the clock was made in France as a commission for a buyer in London, where in 1560 there were very few, if any, native clockmakers.

The rear dial is engraved with degree scales, a Julian calendar appropriate for 1560, and the signs of the zodiac. The upper central area has a circular table showing lunar and solar cycles of nineteen and twenty-eight years and a table of relevant Dominical letters. To each side scales show unequal hours. Below the centre a shadow square, for use in conjunction with the alidade, or sight, allows the instrument to be used to demonstrate angular measuring in surveying.

Octavius Morgan purchased the clock in 1850 from a London watch-maker. Before that, it had an illustrious history, being owned by the eighteenth-century astronomer and mathematician James Ferguson. He described it in his 'Commonplace Book' and executed a splendid drawing to accompany his description. He notes that his good friend Thomas Mudge gave him the clock and compares the wheel-work to his own:

> I confess that I was very glad to find I had hit upon the same sort of motions in a clock as had been done 215 years ago, but of which I knew nothing until I had seen it in this clock. And it is abundantly plain, that by comparing the wheelwork and numbers of teeth in this and in mine, I have not (and indeed could not have) taken the hint from this ancient German performance.

Octavius Morgan Bequest
(Reg. 1888,12–1.101)

Jean de la Garde, senior

Armillary clock
Blois, c.1550
Height 37 cm, width 15 cm, depth 15 cm

By the middle of the sixteenth century, clockmaking was flourishing not only in the German states but also in France. One of the great centres of clockmaking was Blois, where technical and decorative skills had reached a very sophisticated level. Alongside more mundane clocks were those made to impress and amaze as well as to tell the time. One such is this armillary clock made in about 1550.

The base-plate is punched underneath with a ribbon bearing the inscription I.DE LA GARDE arranged around the word BLOYS. The maker, Jean de la Garde senior, remains an undocumented character except for a reference to his wife who is described in 1552 as 'godmother, Marguerite, widow of Jehan de la Garde, clockmaker'.

From the plain gilded-brass base a central triple column rises to support the horizon and meridian rings. The horizon ring is marked 'SEPTENTRION, ORIENS, MERIDIES and OCCIDENS' for north, east, south and west. The horizon and meridian rings carry a revolving armillary sphere with a terrestrial globe in the middle. The base of the clock and its three-column support have undergone much restoration, probably during the nineteenth century, but the original base-plate with the maker's punch-mark survives.

The armillary sphere consists of a number of connected rings representing the north and south polar circles, the two tropics of Capricorn and Cancer, the horizon and two circles for the solstices and equinoxes. In the middle is a wide ecliptic band pierced with the signs of the zodiac. At various points around the sphere there are star pointers indicating the positions of twenty-three major stars. The original chapter ring and hand are missing from the very top of the armillary sphere.

In the middle of the armillary is a terrestrial globe with geographical information based closely on the Parisian 1531 map of the world by Oronce Finé. This globe contains a clock mechanism which drives the rotating armillary. It strikes the hours on a bell and indicates the time on the top dial. The terrestrial globe is fixed, with the armillary sphere rotating around it once per day. Around the ecliptic, sun and moon globes rotate in relation to it, the sun once per year and the moon once per lunar month.

Even with later repairs and restorations, this clock is a magnificent example of the highly developed clockmaking skills which had become established in France by the mid-sixteenth century. It displays an ingenious combination of mechanical skills and astronomical knowledge of the time and would have been worthy of a place in the collection of any nobleman of the time.

Octavius Morgan bequest
(Reg. 1888,12–1.116)

Lucas Weydman

Tabernacle clock
Krakow, 1648
Height 47 cm, width 28 cm, depth 28 cm

By the mid-seventeenth century, the art of making finely-decorated clocks had spread from the south German centres of Augsburg, Nuremberg and Munich as far east as Poland. One particularly popular type was the tabernacle clock, like this fine example. It is designed to strike the hours and the quarters but is also rare in having a secondary mechanism, housed in the base, to strike the hour again after the main striking, as a reminder. This system, known as *Nachschlag* in sixteenth-century Germanic clocks, is found to this day in church clocks in France and Italy.

The case of this magnificent clock is finely engraved around the base, with scenes depicting Adam and Eve in the Garden of Eden and their temptation and fall, each accompanied by a Latin text. The front dial plate is engraved with a townscape incorporating four angels and the signature '*Lucas Weydman Cracow* A.D. 1648'. The two side doors are inset, most unusually, with engraved glass panels. Hugh Tait, in *Clocks and Watches,* an earlier survey of the Museum's collection, discussed these panels and identified their origins in J. Tipotius' *Symbola Divina et Humana,* first published in Prague in 1601. He also identified the symbolism of the image of the two heads in the clouds blowing out a candle as a reference to the death of King Wladyslaw IV Wasa in 1648. The recurring theme of large birds on the roofs of buildings, engraved on the various dials, may be a reference to the same theme. One of the glass panels is original but the other, which is much clearer and flatter, is likely to be a nineteenth-century replacement.

Within the case is a two-stage movement. The upper stage has undergone considerable alteration, but originally had a going train with verge escapement and balance control. There were two trains for striking the hours and the quarters and an alarm. The base of the clock contains a second hour-striking train, released by the main hour-striking mechanism to repeat the hour a few moments after the first striking sequence for anyone who failed to count the first time.

The main dial on the front has a single steel hand to show the time. An outer ring is marked for minutes 5–60 and also I–IIII for the quarters. Within this is a silver chapter ring with hours I–XII and T-shaped half-hour marks. In the middle of this chapter ring is a rotating dial consisting of three overlaid discs: the one at the bottom calibrated 1–12 for alarm setting, the middle disc numbered 1–30 for the age of the moon, and the upper disc with two hands; the larger to show the time, and the smaller to indicate the age of the moon. In the upper disc is an aperture which reveals the phase of the moon and in the very centre is a simple aspectarium showing the astrological relationship between the moon and the sun. The lower silver dial at the front has a single hand which rotates once in twenty-four hours to show Bohemian or Italian hours, where each day begins at sunset. The centre is engraved with a view of a town, with a large bird flying over it.

The back of the clock is engraved with a townscape in which stand depictions of St Barbara, carrying her attribute, a tower, and St Anne holding a book with large letters. In the background, on the horizon, is a

tower with a large bird on the roof. There are two silver dials, the one to the right, numbered 1–12, shows the position of the hour-striking count-wheel. In the middle it is engraved with a townscape and a bird. The left dial is numbered I–IIII to show the position of the quarters count-wheel and is also engraved with a townscape. There are three winding holes and also smaller holes for releasing the striking trains to synchronize them with the time shown on the main front dial.

Repair marks on the inside provide evidence that the clock was in France between 1686 and 1836 but it is thought that it may have originally have belonged to King Jan Kazimierz II Wasa (1609–1672) crowned in 1648 following the death of his brother Wladyslaw IV.

Presented by Octavius Morgan, 1867
(Reg. 1867,7–16.4)

Anonymous

Miniature silver and enamel cased table clock
Augsburg, c.1580
Height 6.5 cm, width 3.7 cm, depth 3.7 cm

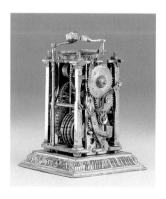

In 1861 Octavius Morgan described this clock as:

A miniature standing clock in a form of square tower ornamented with pilasters at the corners supporting minute obelisks. The height of the clock is only one and three quarter inches and the width of each side one and one quarter inches. The case is of silver gilt enriched with enamel, representing hunting subjects with boars, stags and other animals. In the movement the wheels and pinions are of steel and the original balance wheel has not been replaced by a pendulum. It goes for 12 hours, strikes and has an alarm. Beneath the hour dial is a smaller circle with a hand to indicate the quarters. It is probably of German work and its date may be about 1600. It is the smallest standard clock I have met with and from its minute size and elegant ornament and condition is an object of much interest.

This charming little clock has a silver-gilt case with four corner pillars topped by obelisk finials. At the top, a gallery surrounds the bell. Originally there would have been a top finial to add proportion to the overall design. The front, back and side panels are enamelled in colours and depict hunting scenes, a typical decoration on metal objects of late sixteenth -century southern Germany. This rare piece has been compared by earlier authors to a superb writing-box by Hans and Elias Lencker with similar scenes, finished in about 1585 and recorded in inventories of the Bavarian Wittelsbach family. A clock so exquisitely decorated would without doubt also have merited inclusion in a princely *Kunstkammer*.

The movement has three gear trains for time indication, hour striking and alarm, arranged between brass plates within an iron frame with square-section iron corner pillars. The wheels are of iron, but the barrels and the fusee are brass, typical for clocks made in the late sixteenth century. There is a verge escapement controlled by a balance wheel housed in the upper part of the clock.

The clock has three dials, two on the front and one at the rear. On the front is the main dial showing the hours with a small subsidiary dial below to indicate the quarters. In the middle is a small dial for alarm setting with four small holes in it to aid turning. The rear dial indicates the last hour struck. Unfortunately none of the three hands is original. There are three winding squares, two at the front and one at the back, to allow this splendid little clock to be wound with a key.

Octavius Morgan bequest
(Reg. 1888,12–1.130)

Anonymous

Milkmaid and cow automaton clock
Poland, c.1580
Height 22 cm, width 25.6 cm, depth 20.6 cm

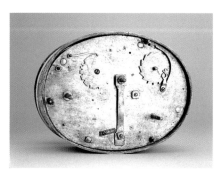

In the last quarter of the sixteenth century the fashion for clocks with automated figures (and for machines which were solely automata) reached its height at the courts of the Holy Roman Empire and with rich customers in the Ottoman Empire. The so-called 'Tribute to the Sublime Gate', which began in 1548 as a payment from the Holy Roman Emperor to Suleiman the Magnificent to prevent an Ottoman invasion of the Empire, produced a demand for such lavish automated clocks and automata. One of the most prolific centres for the manufacture of these wonderful toys was Augsburg in south Germany. Although unsigned, this particular clock is a rare surviving example of a milkmaid and cow automaton with clock, made in Poland very much in the Augsburg style.

The oval case is engraved around with strapwork, foliage and fruits, typical of the last quarter of the sixteenth century. There are two original dials on the top, the first an hour dial with chapters I–XII and 13–24 and T-shaped half-hour marks. Above this a farmer stands and indicates the time with a long staff as he revolves. The second original dial is engraved with foliate scrolls and originally had a hand with which the striking and automaton functions were set in motion. The third dial is a later addition, used to regulate the clock, and was probably added when the escapement was converted to balance spring.

A milkmaid sits on a milking-stool next to the cow. The cow's eyes move from side to side, their motion taken from the oscillating balance in the clock movement below. When the hand on the top is turned, the milkmaid 'milks' the cow, and liquid held in a reservoir inside the cow's body is pumped into a bucket (a later replacement). A hole in the top of the cow's back allows use of a small funnel to fill the reservoir with milk.

Inside the case is an oval movement with, unusually, a steel back plate and brass front plate. All the wheels are of steel but the fusee and the barrels are of brass, a typical arrangement for a late sixteenth-century clock. There are two gear trains, one for timekeeping and one for hour-striking, controlled by a count-wheel and released by a twelve-point star wheel mounted on the dial wheel under the top plate, which rotates once in twelve hours.

This piece is a rare survivor. There are few examples of sixteenth century automaton clocks known today and most of them are in the form of lions or mythical beasts. This is the only one known with a bucolic theme and a very rare example of a clock which pumps liquid. In its time it must have seemed a magical entertainment.

Octavius Morgan Bequest
(Reg. 1888,12–1.122)

Lois François

Table clock
France, c.1550
Height 17.5 cm, width 8.2 cm

In this rather charming little example of a French spring-driven clock of about 1550, the dial is mounted vertically so that it can be easily seen. A characteristic found in the small surviving group of French clocks of this type is that the striking and going trains are mounted one above the other, an arrangement which is not found in the Germanic tradition. In this example, the striking train is at the bottom and the going train at the top. This arrangement allows the dial to be placed centrally in the front of the case rather than at the bottom, but also means that the arbor for the hammer has to be long, and pass up from the bottom of the movement to above the top plate where the bell is located. The movement is made mostly of iron, with elegantly shaped pillars separating the three movement plates. There is a verge escapement and the controlling device here is an oscillating wheel balance. The wheels, pillars and plates are all made from iron but the fusee and barrel are made from brass. While brass was commonly used as a metal for case decoration, where it was well suited for engraving and gilding, it was not thought strong enough in components which would be subjected to stress, such as wheels, pinions and movement plates.

The hexagonal case is pierced around the top with a series of holes to allow the sound of the bell to escape and has a later ribbed domed top with a turned finial above to enclose the bell, added in the nineteenth century. Around the case, five panels are engraved with depictions of Mars, Mercury, Jupiter, Venus and Saturn, ruling planets for days of the week, with the sun engraved on the dial panel. Hugh Tait in *Clocks and Watches* has associated these engravings with designs by a master engraver with the initials IB and dated 1528. Copies survive today in the Department of Prints & Drawings in The British Museum and a close comparison shows just how carefully the engraver of the clock panels copied from the originals. Such designs were relied upon by engravers whose imagination might have been less fertile than that of the great designers. Perhaps one of the most celebrated of French designers of the sixteenth century was Etienne Delaune, and certainly one of the more copied engraver/designers of the Germanic tradition was Virgil Solis.

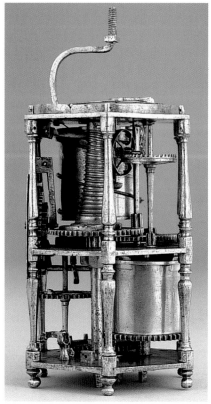

The clock is inscribed LOIS F on the base, a shortened form of Lois François, a Parisian clockmaker working in the mid-sixteenth century.

Presented by Mr H.J. Pfungst in 1902
(Reg. 1902,4–18.1)

Bartholomew Newsam

Table clock
London, c.1585
Height 16.8 cm, width 7.1 cm, depth 7 cm

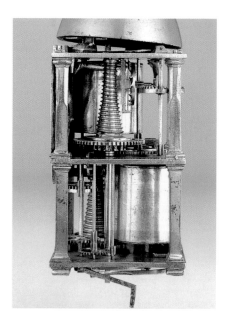

Bartholomew Newsam was almost certainly from York, where others in his family lived. He became a prominent clockmaker to the Royal household in London towards the end of Queen Elizabeth's reign, when he took over the appointment of Clockmaker to the Queen after the death of Nicholas Ourseau. Newsam is known to have been in London from as early as 1568, from which time he leased property in the Strand, near Somerset House. He died in 1593 and in his will he left his tools and workshop equipment as follows:

> to John Newsom my best vice save one a beckhorne to stand upon borde, a great fore hammer and to hand hammers a grete longe beckhorne in my backe shoppe, and all the rest of my tooles I give unto Edward Newsom my sonne with condition that he become a Clockmaker as I am, yf not I will the foresaid tooles to be sould by my executors or executrix and the mony therof cominge to be imployed towardes his bringinge upp to some other profession wherunto his mynde shall best serve.

Three clocks by Newsam are known to survive, one of which is this gilt-copper spring-driven table clock dating from about 1585. Unfortunately, the engraving on the case has been badly rubbed, and subsequent re-gilding has done little to enhance its clarity. It is still possible to discern the subjects of the decoration and identify them as derived from designs by the great French engraver Etienne Delaune (1518–1595). His designs were popular in late sixteenth and early seventeenth century watch-case decoration. The quality of the engraving, however, suggests that the case was made and decorated in England rather than imported from France, where far finer and more artistic work was being executed at this time. While this little clock has engraved decoration in the French manner, the dome is perhaps more readily associated with pierced tops of Flemish origin. An interesting feature is the compass housed in the drum-shaped canister at the very top of the clock, which would seem in this context to serve no purpose.

The movement also shows a strong French influence. It was common practice in France for small vertical table clocks to have their movements constructed in such a way that the two separate gear trains for time-keeping and striking were arranged one above the other, the timekeeping train at the top, and the striking train at the bottom. With the bell usually located in the dome at the top, this necessitated a long hammer arbor passing up from the bottom to the top. Another feature commonly found in French work and indeed also present in this clock are the small doors in the sides of the case which allow the state of winding of the fusees to be observed. The clock has just one dial, marked for hours I–XII, and with star-shaped half-hour marks, all on a raised ring. The single steel hand is a later replacement.

Octavius Morgan Bequest
(Reg. 1888,12–1.126)

Anonymous

Table clock 'Orpheus'
Augsburg?, c.1580
Height 22 cm, width 8 cm, depth 8 cm

Dating from about 1575, this clock has its origins in south Germany, probably Augsburg itself. Although unsigned, it is one of a series of eleven superb table clocks known as the 'Orpheus' clocks, so called because the legend of Orpheus was the subject chosen for the decoration of the case bands. This square-cased example has cast and chased decoration of the highest quality, taken from designs by Virgil Solis and thought to be the work of Hans Kels, showing Orpheus charming the animals in the forest.

The fact that the cast panels appear on ten different clocks, but are nevertheless clearly from the same mould, suggests that clockmakers could buy strips of the casting and use it to form cases of either round or square shape and perhaps produce clocks in some form of batch production.

The clock mechanism is made entirely from iron and has gear trains for time indication and hour-striking, but has the added sophistication that the clock can be made to strike either in the twelve-hour system (1–12 twice per day) or the six-hour (1–6 four times per day). To enhance the appearance of the back plate of the clock when the case is opened for winding, there is a false plate of gilt-brass profusely engraved with foliate scrolls. As well as this, all the iron parts including the plates, wheels, arbors and pillars of the movement are burnished, a finish which may well be original and intended to enhance the appearance of the movement but also perhaps to provide a more rust-resistant surface.

Above the dial is a detachable alarm mechanism released by the hour hand as it turns. In Germanic spring-driven table clocks of the sixteenth century it is not uncommon to find a detachable alarm mechanism which could be attached to the top of the clock when an alarm function was needed. The mechanism is simply clipped on to the top of the clock in a position where the release lever is directly over the desired alarm time. The alarm is then set off when the hour hand arrives at that position and trips the lever. This simple device consists of a mainspring and short train of wheels, which drive a crown wheel and verge escapement. A hammer is mounted on the end of the verge to sound the alarm on the bell at the top. This simple mechanism allowed the clock to perform as a horizontal table clock in normal use but also as an alarm clock when required.

Octavius Morgan Bequest
(Reg. 1888,12–1.102)

Anonymous

Masterpiece clock
Augsburg, *c.*1650
Height 70.5 cm, width 41 cm

A clock which shows the time both in the great and small clock i.e., the 12-hour and 24-hour system. It should show the times of sunrise and sunset and also show the position of the sun and moon in the zodiac throughout the year. It should strike the quarter hours and the full hours in both 1–12 and 1–24 hour systems.

These were the basic requirements for a 'masterpiece' clock in Augsburg when this clock was made. In order to qualify as a master clockmaker, a craftsman had first to serve his apprenticeship and then follow it with a period serving different masters as a journeyman. The total period of servitude varied but usually amounted to about seven or eight years. When this was completed, he would be able to apply for permission to submit a masterpiece, which had to be of suitable quality to satisfy the masters of the guild who judged it. For the completion of this work the aspiring clockmaker would be given six months, during which time he would not be expected to do any other work.

This spectacular piece has all the characteristics of such a masterpiece clock but suffers from the fact that, although done in a most sympathetic way, the whole of the movement was removed and replaced by a much simpler mechanism in France in the nineteenth century. Many of the dials no longer function. In spite of this rather draconian alteration, the clock is still a superb example of the clockmaker's, or perhaps more specifically, the case-maker's art of mid-seventeenth century Augsburg.

The hexagonal structure is made from gilded-brass, silvered brass and, in part, solid silver components and is designed to impress with such an array of indications that there can be little that is left to the imagination. The original concave base is decorated with flowers and foliage but the proportion is now distorted by the addition of a wide 'skirt' to increase its depth to provide clearance for the nineteenth-century pendulum. Sitting horizontally at the top of the base is a revolving calendar ring, which is engraved with the date, the Dominical Letters, the saints' days and the months with the number of days in each. The dates at which the zodiacs change are also marked.

Above this, the clock is hexagonal and each facet has a dial or dials as follows:

- The main front facet has two dials. The upper dial is in the form of an astrolabe with a pierced rete or spider engraved with the ecliptic, showing the signs and degrees of the zodiac and with pointers showing the position of nineteen stars with their magnitudes. The time is shown by a centrally-mounted arm with a sun effigy at its end, registering against a silver chapter ring engraved I-XII-I-XII. At the centre, the lunar hand has a disc engraved with an aspectarium and pierced with a round aperture to show the phase of the moon. The moon's age is shown by a pointer on the lunar hand which indicates against a scale of 1-29 1/2 on the solar disc below it. Underneath the rete is a plate engraved with celestial coordinates for use at about 50° north, the latitude of Krakow. On this disc there are also curved lines to show unequal or seasonal hours.

The lower silver dial is engraved I-XII for the 'small' hours on a chapter ring which surrounds a revolving disc numbered 1–12. This disc is turned to set the required alarm time against the tail of the blued steel hand which indicates the time.

- The facet at the rear of the clock has two dials, the upper one with a sunrise-sunset / daylight-darkness indiactor consisting of two overlapping discs, one of silver and one of blued-steel which automatically change their relative positions through the year. Around this a gilt-brass ring is engraved 1–24 and the gilt hand which indicates against it shows Nuremberg or Bohemian hours where the day began at sunset or sunrise respectively. The hand would have been manually adjusted periodically as the times of sunrise and sunset changed during the year. On the outside, the silver chapter ring and the outer gilt chapter ring allow the concentric blued-steel hands to show mean time in the 12- and 24-hour systems.

  The lower dial is engraved with the signs of the zodiac and a dial which shows the length of daylight from eleven hours to twenty hours, according to the time of year and the latitude.

- Two dials show the positions of the 12- and 24-hour count-wheels to help when synchronizing the striking with the time shown on the dials.

- Two dials, the upper one for switching the striking between the 12- and 24-hour systems and the lower one to show the day of the week.

- A dial to show the position of the quarter-strike count-wheel, also provided to aid synchronization. There is a small hole in this dial which allows a pin to be inserted to release the striking.

- Two dials, the upper one numbered 1–8 and probably originally connected to a hog's bristle regulator acting on the balance, and a lower dial engraved with a 28-year cycle of Dominical Letters with double letters for the leap years.

All the facets of this level are lavishly engraved with realistic flowers in the areas around the various dials. Two of the panels are punched with a pine-cone, the town mark of Augsburg, perhaps confirming the status of the clock as a masterpiece. Above the dial level the clock takes the form of two hexagonal boxes with profusely pierced and engraved gilt-brass and silver panels which originally housed the bells. The corners of the clock are in the form of highly ornate buttresses, which begin at the top of the base and rise up through the levels to converge at the top where they support an armillary sphere. These buttresses are in the form of dolphins at the bottom and eagle heads at the top of the dial level. From here, spires rise up to create an elaborate and highly decorative effect.

Ilbert Collection
(Reg. CAI–2129)

Johann Buschmann
(attributed)

Table clock with cross-beat escapement
Augsburg, c.1650
Height 49 cm, width 32.7 cm, depth 23.3 cm

Johann Buschmann the elder (1591–1662) was one of the leading clock-makers in Augsburg during the first half of the seventeenth century. A rare insight into his character exists in a description of him by Johann Martin Hirt, the son-in-law of the famous art agent Philipp Hainhofer (1578–1647) who said of Buschmann that he was never without a mug of beer on his bench and that he always made sure the Duke's latest order was being worked on when he saw him (Hirt) coming along the street to visit the workshop to check on progress. In spite of his liking for beer, there is no doubt that Buschmann was one of the most talented makers of his time.

When this clock was made, in the 1650s, the most recent refinement in clockmaking was the cross-beat escapement. Although this escapement is commonly attributed to the great clockmaker Jost Bürgi, it was actually invented by Jacques Besson, who published it in 1569. However, it was Bürgi who developed it and used it with great success in his precision regulators made for use by astronomers. In support of a Buschmann attribution to this clock are some fascinating drawings now in the Herzog August Bibliothek in Wolfenbüttel, including one of a clock with cross-beat escapement not unlike this example.

Of simple design, the clock has a typical Augsburg ebony base marked with a pine-cone, the mark of that city. Here, Buschmann puts the escapement to good use with a superbly made steel escape wheel with three-hundred teeth. Wheels such as this show well the accomplishment of the best German clockmakers in this period. To power the escapement, Buschmann has used another technical innovation also popularized by Jost Bürgi, the spring remontoire. A small secondary spring is designed to power the escapement directly and is periodically rewound by a large mainspring housed in the ebony base of the clock. Its purpose is to obviate the excessive differences in the power output of the mainspring should it be directly used to impulse the escapement. Sadly, the escapement and the astrolabic dial of this clock are now missing, except for the engraved plate which should underly the rete (as pp. 24, 42). The small dial at the bottom shows the days of the week and has an aperture to show the moon's age.

Purchased in 1973
(Reg. 1973,2–2.1)

Isaac Habrecht

Carillon clock
Strasbourg, 1589
Height 140 cm, width 38.5 cm, depth 38.5 cm

This clock is undoubtedly one of the most important surviving examples of Renaissance clockwork. It was made by Isaac Habrecht in Strasbourg in 1589. Its design was conceived in imitation of the great astronomical clock in the cathedral there, a clock which Habrecht had completed in 1574 under the direction of Conrad Dasypodius, a mathematician at Strasbourg University, who had been commissioned to design a new clock for the cathedral. This domestic version of the cathedral clock is one of two surviving examples by Habrecht (the other is in Rosenborg Castle in Copenhagen). It stands more than five feet tall and is a magnificent example of the clockmaker and engraver's art, combining a superb mechanism with a magnificently engraved case of the finest quality.

As well as the two main dials which show the time separately in hours and minutes, there is an annual calendar at the bottom with astronomical indications in the middle, showing the position of the sun and moon in the zodiac throughout the year, as well as the age and phase of the moon. Above the time dials, a carousel shows the days of the week, each personified by its ruling deity riding in a chariot pulled by fabulous beasts. In the stage above, in its original conception, the Three Magi processed before the seated Virgin and Child as the clock played music after the hour was struck. Now the procession consists of small, rather badly-cast angels who replace the original figures. Above this, the Four Ages of Man strike the quarters on a bell, but here one of the Four Ages has been replaced with one of the Magi figures from the stage below, who now strikes the bell with his incense jar. At the top the figure of Christ appears through a doorway, and at the hour the figure of Death strikes the passing hours on a large bell. When the hours are struck, the two small silver putti on the front move their arms, one turns an hour glass while the other raises and lowers a sickle (formerly a sceptre, now missing). The automaton figures are an impressive blend of the religious and the secular.

In addition to striking the hours and quarters, the clock plays music at each hour; a setting of the 'Vater Unser' first published in *Geistliche Lieder auffs neu gebessert und gemehrt* (Leipzig, 1539). The clock is housed in a fine gilt-metal case engraved with Faith, Hope and Charity on the right, Wisdom, Fortitude and Justice on the left, and the Three Fates, Glotto, Lachesis and Atropos on the back. On the front, the emblems of the four ancient empires of Greece, Rome, Asia and Persia surround the calendar dial, and the four seasons fill the spandrel spaces around the main dial. In addition to these lavish decorations, the clock is also adorned with biblical quotations.

The movement consists of four weight-driven gear trains, for time indication, quarter strike, hour strike and music, all contained in a massive steel frame. The wheels are made of brass which was, by 1589, becoming more commonly used. In later years, perhaps at the beginning of the eighteenth century, the clock was converted from its original balance-controlled verge escapement to have the new pendulum control in order to greatly improve its timekeeping.

It was long thought that this clock had been made for Pope Sixtus V, but the music played by it and the engraved subjects which decorate it suggest very strongly that it must have been destined for a Protestant prince. The attribution to the Pope was based on the fact that it is known that the clock was in the Papal collections in the early nineteenth century. That a clock playing music written by Martin Luther should be commissioned by a Pope in the sixteenth century is inconceivable. One possible explanation for the existence of the clock in Rome is that during the Thirty Years War (1618–48) the library of the Elector of the Palatine in Heidelberg was seized as spoils of war by the Papal army and taken to Rome. Later it was placed in the possession of the King Willem I of the Netherlands as surety for a loan that the King gave to Herman Kessels (1794–1851) in 1829. Kessels was raising money to fund the exhibition of a massive whale carcass. In 1848, however, the clock appeared in London where it was exhibited at the Royal Society. It was here that Octavius Morgan saw it. In 1853, Morgan wrote the following letter to Augustus Wollaston Franks at the British Museum:

> I have again inspected the clock and fear that I must give it up from the difficulty of finding a place for it in my house as well as the removal of so large and heavy a thing to so great a distance – but I do so with great regret – for it would be an invaluable addition to my collection. I believe it to be the finest and grandest specimen of ancient clockwork in the world. I mean of course of a moveable kind for I except such horological structures as those in the cathedrals of Strasbourg and Lubeck. It is a genuine production of the date and was made by the same artist who made the Strasbourg clock and somewhat in imitation of it. I have never seen anything like it to my recollection of clocks in the Museums of Brunswick, Hesse-Cassel, Dresden or Vienna. I should like to see it in our national Museum for it is more fit for that than a private collection and I am inclined to think that if placed there and kept in order would be one of the most curious and interesting objects there. I have the refusal of it for one hundred pounds which from its being an unique specimen and so fine and curious a thing I do not think much out of the way for when I saw it some years ago I was asked four hundred pounds for it. I am obliged to give an answer by Tuesday as other parties are after it – some dealers are I believe willing to give that sum for it.

Unfortunately the Museum was not willing to part with one hundred pounds for the clock. Morgan bought it for himself and took it back to his house, The Friars, in Newport, South Wales. It stood at the bottom of the main staircase until his death in 1888, when it was bequeathed to The British Museum along with the rest of his amazing collection of clocks and watches.

Octavius Morgan Bequest
(Reg. 1888,12–1.100)

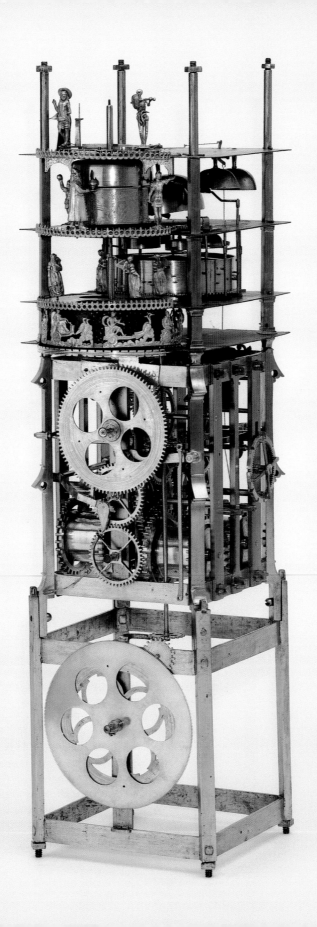

Hans Schlottheim

Automaton clock in the form of a ship or nef
Augsburg, *c.*1585
Height 104 cm, length 78.5 cm, width 20.3 cm (excluding cannons)

A gilded Ship or Nef, skilfully made, with a quarter and full hour striking clock, which is to be wound every 24 hours. Above are three masts, in the crow's nests of which sailors revolve and strike the quarters and hours with hammers on the bells. Inside, the Holy Roman Emperor sits on the imperial throne, and in front of him pass the seven electors with heralds, paying homage as they receive their fiefs. Furthermore ten trumpeters and a kettle drummer alternately announce the banquet. Also a drummer and three guardsmen, and sixteen small cannon, eleven of which may be loaded and fire automatically. With its protective case, it stands on a long green table cloth.

This description of a ship automaton, recently discovered by John Leopold, former curator of horology at the British Museum, in the inventories of the *Kunstkammer* of the Elector of Saxony in Dresden, could easily refer to a magnificent 'nef' made by Hans Schlottheim of Augsburg in about 1585, which is now in The British Museum collections. It has a small clock, showing hours and minutes on a beautiful silver dial with coloured enamel floral motifs. Sailors wielding hammers in the crow's nests strike the hours and quarters. However, the machine is not essentially a clock, but a magnificent and ingenious automaton designed to announce a banquet by travelling independently along a table. As it went, a small regal or pipe organ would play a tune and drumsticks would play on a skin stretched across the base of the ship's hull. While all this was going on, the tops of the fore and mizzen masts would twirl round. As part of the entertainment, the Electors of the Holy Roman Empire, preceded by two heralds, processed and each made a small bow before the Holy Roman Emperor, Rudolf II, seated on a throne beneath a canopy. The ship moved on again accompanied by the music and drumming and as a grand finale to entertain the guests, it fired the main cannon in the bowsprit, which then ignited a fast-burning fuse that burnt quickly round the hull, firing off the other cannons in turn to finish its performance in a wonder of noise and smoke.

Hans Schlottheim was born some time between 1544 and 1547, the son of a clockmaker from Naumburg in Saxony. From as early as 1567 he lived in Augsburg. Although nothing is known of his apprenticeship, it is recorded that he was a journeyman clockmaker in the workshop of Jeremias Metzger in the 1570s. On 20 December 1573 he married Ursula Geiger, widow of the master locksmith Hans Schitterer. By this marriage he obtained his 'smith's eligibility' or *Schmiedegerechtigkeit* and was thus able to begin working in his own right within the Augsburg Clockmakers' Guild, where he became a master clockmaker in 1576. In 1586 Schlottheim became a 'guard' within the guild, with responsibility for supervising the quality of the work of the other Augsburg clock makers. It was in 1586 that he was given permission to work for a year at the Imperial Court in Prague. In subsequent years he again left Augsburg to work for the Prince Elector of Saxony in Dresden in 1589 and 1593. Schlottheim died in 1625; his second wife, Euphrosina Osswald, having been described as a widow in the tax registers for 1626.

Schlottheim is also renowned for a number of other clocks and
automata, including in 1577 the first public clock to be installed in
Augsburg that struck the hours and quarters. He also made two other
nefs; one in the Musée National de la Renaissance in Écouen and one in
the Kunsthistorisches Museum in Vienna. As well as these, Schlottheim
is known to have made the 'Trumpeter Automaton' in 1582 for Wilhelm
V, Duke of Bavaria, who presented it to Archduke Ferdinand of the Tyrol,
and which is now in the Kunsthistorisches Museum in Vienna. A further
clock known as the 'Christmas Nativity' automaton, described in the
Dresden *Kunstkammer* inventory of 1 January 1589, was intended for the
Ottoman Emperor in about 1584. It was destroyed in 1945 and now only
survives as a fragment in the Mathematisch-Physikalischer Salon in
Dresden. In 1588 he created two crayfish in red-painted copper, one of

them now also in the Mathematisch-Physikalischer Salon, Dresden. In addition to these, Schlottheim made a trumpeter automaton in 1589 for the Duchess of Graz and in about 1600, a clock with a rolling ball called 'The Tower of Babel' now in the Grünes Gewölbe, Dresden. Lastly there is 'The Triumph of Bacchus' automaton, which he made in about 1605 and which is also in the Kunsthistorisches Museum in Vienna.

The British Museum nef was purchased by Octavius Morgan in 1866 and presented to the Museum. In that year he wrote:

> My dear Franks, I have as you know, lately purchased a wonderful clock in the form of a medieval ship having several automaton figures which move with the clockwork. My intention was to have added it to my collection of ancient clocks down here but the difficulty and trouble of getting it here when cleaned and properly set to right as it requires and especially the great risk of its sustaining injury in the journey and frequent moving have made me determined to offer it as a present to the British Museum, if the Trustees shall be pleased to accept it. For I consider it to be an object of such great curiosity and interest, independently of its being so beautiful a piece of work, and such a fine specimen of the mechanism of the sixteenth century that I really think it is a pity that so fine a thing should be concealed in a private house instead of forming part of a public collection as it would be if received into the British Museum where it would be appreciated . . . Yours very truly, Octavius Morgan.[*]

Sadly, the years have not been kind to this nef and now none of it functions and nearly all the original figures are missing. Those on the main deck are all copies of an original standing at the edge of the rear deck and many others are no longer present.

Presented by Octavius Morgan in 1866
(Reg. 1866,10–30.1)

Nicholas Vallin

Carillon clock
London, 1598
Height 59 cm, width 26 cm, depth 23.3 cm

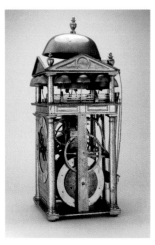

Nicholas Vallin was a refugee who spent time in Spain with the Emperor Charles V and came to London from Brussels with his father John, a native of Ryssel (Lille). In the 1580s they were living in the parish of St Ann's, Blackfriars, and were members of the Dutch Church in Austin Friars. The first definite date for Nicholas is the record of his marriage at the Dutch Church in June 1590 to Elizabeth Rendtmeesters from Brussels. Nicholas's life in England was short, for he died in the 1603 plague along with his father, two of his three daughters and two journeyman clockmakers who were working for him at the time.

Vallin's most impressive surviving clock is undoubtedly this magnificent musical weight-driven chamber clock, dated 1598, which strikes the hours and plays music at each quarter. For many years it played rather 'unmusical' melodies, installed fairly recently. So that it can give a better account of its original sound, it has been restored to play music contemporary with its date. The pin barrel which operates the hammers has a wooden centre covered with a brass drum drilled all round to enable the tunes to be easily changed. Following restoration the clock now plays tunes taken from the Fitzwilliam Virginal Book of 1612. A short flourish is played at the first quarter, followed by 'Paiana' by John Bull at the half hour, 'The Bells' by William Byrd at the third quarter and John Dowland's 'His Golden Locks' on the hour, this last piece originally spoken by Sir Henry Lee on his retirement in 1590 as Queen Elizabeth's Champion.

The clock was made to be mounted on a bracket high on the wall, and the musical quarters are played on thirteen bells. The hours are announced to the whole household on the impressive bell at the top. Its construction is characteristic of Flemish work of the period with the gear wheels running in plates at right-angles to the dial and with the count-wheel for the striking mounted on one side. The plates in which the wheels run are held in an iron frame with four corner pillars with gilt-metal capitals and plinths which support the upper and lower plates on to which the bearing plates are fixed. In essence this is the forerunner of the design for the lantern clock, which became a standard English clock in the second quarter of the seventeenth century. The dial is engraved with an architectural design and signed N VALLIN 1598. Above the main frame is a gallery that provides space for the balance wheel and above that the musical bells are clustered beneath classical pediments. The four corners and the hour bell are topped by gilded brass urn finials. The dial has undergone some alteration and now has a more recent chapter ring and hands but the under-dial work appears to be original, suggesting that this clock is an early example of one with concentric hour and minute hands.

Ilbert Collection
(Reg. CAI–2139)

Samuel Haug

Horizontal table clock with grande-sonnerie striking and alarm
Augsburg, c.1620
Height 9.2 cm, width 17.2 cm, depth 17.2 cm

Samuel Haug was one of the more accomplished makers in south Germany in the early part of the seventeenth century. He was born in Augsburg in about 1579 and became a master watch- and clockmaker in the Augsburg Guild in 1612. He is listed in the guild register in 1619 as being aged forty and he died in 1637. This clock is punched with Haug's mark SA:HA.

At first glance this looks like a standard horizontal table clock of the period, but closer inspection shows that it is much more sophisticated than it first appears and also that it was modernized some time after it was made. As well as showing the time, the clock has an alarm and strikes the hours and quarters in the grande-sonnerie manner, which means that it strikes the quarter and the hour on two bells at every quarter. Such a system is normally associated with clocks made after the introduction of the rack-striking mechanism in the 1670s, but here the grande-sonnerie system is achieved by using a very finely-made steel count-wheel mounted beneath the dial. The quality of this wheel alone, which would have challenged even good craftsmen, shows the level of skill to which Haug aspired. It is cut with very fine teeth around the inside of the wheel that mesh with the gear train pinion that drives it. Around the outside it is divided into groups of raised sections with a slot cut at the end of each. The slots are arranged in groups of four which get progressively further apart, so that the count-wheel controls the striking of the hours and the groups of four slots allow the clock to strike the hour at each quarter in an increasing progression 1–24. For quarters I–III the clock strikes the quarter followed by the preceding hour, but at the fourth quarter the new hour is struck. To achieve this, Haug utilized three striking trains, one for the quarters, one for the hours at quarters I–III and a separate train for the full hour at the hour.

Improvements were made to the clock in about 1700 when a more fashionable silver chapter ring and dial were fitted and the movement was modified by the addition of a balance spring. This latter improvement would have been carried out in order to bring the performance of the clock up to the new standards achieved following the introduction of the balance spring in 1675. It was probably also then that the silver mounts were added to what was originally a plain gilt-brass case. Such improvements to clocks have often been scorned but in reality the modernisation of old clocks often led to their continued use which has allowed them to survive until today.

Octavius Morgan Bequest
(Reg. 1888,12–1.111)

Leonard Tennant

Turret clock
London, c.1610
Height 56.5 cm, width 44 cm, depth 56 cm

To this day, the first maker of a mechanical clock and the place and date where it was made remains a mystery. There is however, documentary evidence for the existence of such clocks at the end of the thirteenth century that provides interesting information regarding the new clocks that were being installed in cathedrals, abbeys and churches around Europe. As early as 1283 a clock is known to have existed in the Priory of the Austin Canons in Dunstable. Two surviving clocks from this embryonic period are those made for Salisbury and Wells Cathedrals in 1386 and 1389 respectively. The former can still be found in the cathedral itself, while the latter is now in the Science Museum in London. They were both made by a group of clockmakers, Johannes and Williemus Vrieman and Johannes Lietyt, invited from Delft in the Low Countries by Bishop Ralph Ergum for the specific purpose of making the clocks, first at Salisbury and then at Wells.

The design of the turret clock changed little over the following three centuries and this particular example from the early seventeenth century has characteristics similar to clocks made for churches in the medieval period. It is a weight-driven clock with two separate gear trains mounted side by side. The going train is controlled by a verge escapement with an oscillating foliot with adjustable weights. The striking train is controlled by a count-wheel mounted within the frame of the clock. Over the years the clock has been modified and restored a number of times, but in its present state it closely resembles its original conception as a seventeenth-century tower clock with verge escapement and weighted foliot. The clock is marked on one of the top frame bars with a scallop shell and is one of a group of seven clocks which have now been identified either with that mark or with a monogram RL, for Robert Ludlam. The scallop-shell clocks were made by a London clockmaker, Leonard Tennant, who was a member of the Joiners' Company. He is known to have been working in 1606 and had a long list of apprentices who were trained by him between 1606 and 1641. Leonard Tennant died in 1646 leaving his 'great anvil and the great Bickhorne and two great vices' to his cousin Joseph Tennant, having been the head of perhaps the most important turret clockmaking business of the first half of the seventeenth century.

This example from Tennant's workshops was installed in Cassiobury Park, a country house near Watford in Hertfordshire. The house was demolished in the early part of the twentieth century and the clock passed into the collector's market. It was finally purchased by the Museum in 1964.

Purchased from James Oakes in 1964
(Reg. 1964,2–3.1)

William Bowyer

Lantern clock
London, c.1630
Height 43.9 cm, width 14.8 cm, depth 14.7 cm

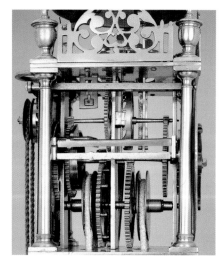

In the sixteenth century, the wall-mounted, weight-driven chamber clock became a relatively common type in the Low Countries (Holland and Flanders). They were mostly constructed from iron and controlled by a balance wheel. The last quarter of the sixteenth century saw an influx into England of Protestant Flemish makers who brought with them their skills in making domestic clocks and, indeed, watches. It comes as no surprise therefore that a style of clock should develop in England which had its origins in the iron chamber clock and such clocks came to be known as lantern clocks. They have also been called 'sheep's-head' clocks and 'Cromwell' clocks, and it was to be a style which would last relatively unchanged for more than 150 years, first in London and other large cities, but increasingly in the country.

Designed to hang on a hook or stand on a bracket high up on the wall, these clocks commonly struck the hours on a large bell mounted at the top of the clock, which could be heard all over the house. The dial has a prominent chapter ring with large numerals and a single hand to register the hours and quarters. Mounted on the outside of the back plate is a small weight-driven alarm mechanism, which is set by turning a small dial in the middle of the main dial. The clock has a verge escapement controlled by a balance wheel and, while nearly all of these clocks were converted to pendulum control in the second half of the seventeenth century, this example has retained its original verge escapement and balance wheel.

William Bowyer lived in Leadenhall Street in the City of London and is thought to have been a member of the Joiners' Company. In 1632, however, he was a founder member of the Clockmakers' Company, becoming an Assistant in 1651 and Warden in 1653, the year in which he is thought to have died. He was principally a clockmaker and a number of his lantern clocks survive, as well as an interesting sundial made in 1630 for Governor John Endicott of Salem, Massachusetts. As a 'great' clockmaker he was probably not involved in the making of watches and there are no surviving examples bearing his name. In 1642 William Bowyer presented to the Clockmakers' Company a 'great chamber clock' in order that he might be excused holding any office in the company. He clearly changed his mind about this in later life when he did indeed hold office and it is likely that it was his death which prevented him becoming Master of the Company.

Ilbert Collection
(Reg. CAI-2094)

Robert Grinkin junior

Horizontal table clock
London, c.1650
Height 7.5 cm, width 12 cm, depth 12 cm

In seventeenth-century England the spring-driven clock was not common until after the introduction of the pendulum in 1657. Before then, the most common domestic clocks were lantern clocks similar to the one by William Bowyer (pp. 62–3). Today, very few of these spring-driven clocks survive, suggesting that they were not made in large numbers. While some of them were lavishly decorated, others such as this one were more austere, perhaps being made with Puritan clients in mind. This particular clock was made by Robert Grinkin, who like his father of the same name was a member of the Blacksmiths' Company. Robert Grinkin junior also became a Free Brother in the Clockmakers' Company in 1632 and served as Warden in 1640 and Master in 1648 and 1654. He lived in Fleet Street and, during his mastership, the Clockmakers' Company Court meetings were held in his house. He died in 1661.

The four lion feet at the corners are the only decoration on the clock. The dial has a chapter ring with hours I–XII and arrowhead half-hour marks surrounding a circle divided into quarter-hours. A central alarm-setting disc is engraved with a seeded rose and numbered 1–11 with a steel pointer at 12 that indicates the time as the disc revolves. The small hand in the middle is for setting the alarm.

The movement is similar to that in a large clock-watch. There are three gear trains, for time keeping, hour striking and alarm, the striking train controlled by a blued-steel count-wheel running under a decorative cover-plate with a small square aperture which shows the last hour struck. Both the striking and alarm trains have geared stop-work. Also on the back plate is a silver disc, engraved with a rose and numbered 1–12, which is turned by a key-operated worm gear. This mechanism allows the owner to regulate the rate of the oscillating balance wheel by increasing or decreasing the power released by the mainspring. The finely pierced and engraved foliate balance cock, also on the back of the movement, is of a form found in watches of the period. The method of fixing is two-fold, firstly by a transverse pin through a stud fixed to the movement plate and secondly by a screw in its foot. The former harks back to the old method and the latter looks forward to a single screw fixing, which would become standard in watchwork.

This design of clock in England came to an abrupt end with the introduction of the pendulum, which necessitated the clock to be arranged vertically for the pendulum to swing and in consequence have a vertical dial like the Edward East clock (pp. 68–9).

The movement is signed on the back plate, *Robert Grinkin Londini*, in a fine cursive script.

Purchased in 1981
(Reg. 1981,7–10.1)

J. Bernard van Stryp

Wall clock
Antwerp, c.1660
Height 25 cm, width 20.3 cm, depth 10.3 cm

In 1657 Christiaan Huygens in The Hague introduced the pendulum as a new and effective device for improving the accuracy of clocks. Before this momentous innovation, clocks were controlled by either a wheel balance or a weighted foliot, neither of which had a natural period of oscillation and so could not provide a constant with which to control the rate. Clocks would vary by as much as half an hour per day and, perhaps more annoyingly, would be erratic in their performance.

The introduction of the pendulum as the controlling device changed matters overnight, and clocks were made which could keep time to within one minute per day. Huygens took out a patent in the Netherlands and employed the clockmaker Salomon Coster to make pendulum clocks. Coster, unfortunately, died soon afterwards in 1659. Huygens failed to obtain patents in either France or England for his new device, and soon all new clocks in these countries were fitted with it. Many older clocks were modernized by the addition of a pendulum.

Bernard van Stryp made this small spring-driven clock in Antwerp (Anvers) in about 1660. In keeping with Huygens' invention, it has a pendulum and cycloidal cheeks on the pendulum suspension. According to Huygens' calculations, the ideal pendulum should swing through a cycloidal path and not a circle. To this end, early pendulum clocks were fitted with cycloidal cheeks which were intended to force the pendulum, suspended from silk threads, into the correct path. So confident were the early makers of these clocks in their ability to keep good time that for a short period they abandoned the use of a fusee in favour of a simple going barrel. The time taken for the pendulum to swing is determined by its length and not the arc through which it swings, within certain limits. This led the makers of early pendulum clocks to believe that the huge differences in power delivered from the mainspring to the escapement between the spring being fully wound and almost unwound could be accommodated by the pendulum simply changing the arc through which it swung depending on the force imparted to it. In practice both this and the use of cycloidal cheeks were found wanting and caused more problems than they solved so that later spring-driven pendulum clocks went back to using a fusee and dispensed with the cycloidal cheeks. The clock is signed *J Bernard Van Stryp fecit Anuers*, on a small silver plaque.

Another interesting feature on this clock, which has a velvet-backed dial popular with Dutch makers, is the method of indicating the time in minutes and seconds. The chapter ring has an outer circle divided for minutes but each minute division has two diagonal lines, which enables the time to be read to a fraction of a minute using only a single hand.

Bequeathed by Mr E.H. Brooks in 1991
(Reg. 1991,10–8.1)

Edward East

Table clock
London, *c.*1665
Height 36.5 cm, width 30.5 cm, depth 16.3 cm

The advent of the pendulum brought in a number of radical changes in the appearance of clocks. In weight-driven clocks, the longcase was the new fashion, but in spring-driven clocks the most obvious change was in the case, where wood was now the favoured material in contrast to the metal of earlier lantern and table clocks. Like the early Dutch pendulum clocks, English clocks of this period had relatively plain cases with all attention focused on the dial.

Edward East was born in 1602 in the village of Southill, Bedfordshire. He lived through virtually the whole of the seventeenth century, surviving plague, fire and revolution. He was apprenticed to Richard Rogers in the Goldsmiths' Company in 1618, and gained his Freedom in that Company in 1627. He was also a founder member of the Clockmakers' Company, being made one of the first assistants in 1632, and served as master in 1645 and 1653. He was also clockmaker to King Charles II from 1660. His business was in Pall Mall in 1632 but was at the 'Musical Clock' in Fleet Street by 1640, and towards the end of his life he worked at the 'Sun outside Temple Bar'. He also had a country residence in Hampton in Middlesex and other property in London, mentioned in his will. He died in 1697 at the age of ninety-five having been the head of one of the most prolific workshops of seventeenth-century London.

This example from East's workshop is austere in style with no superfluous decoration. The case is of plain ebony-veneered oak and the only ornament on the clock is an engraved seeded rose in the centre of an otherwise plain matted dial. The chapter ring is silvered to give a sharp contrast to the matted dial centre and to make the dark blued-steel hands stand out for ease of reading. The clock can be locked to limit access; children were clearly not expected to meddle with time.

The movement is typical of East's early pendulum clocks with large brass plates separated by finely-made baluster pillars and it displays interesting features. The plates are pinned at the back and the going train does not have a centrally-running wheel. The use of a centre-wheel, turning once per hour and carrying a minute hand, had not yet become standard practice. Instead, drive to the hands is taken from the extended second-wheel arbor, which carries a pinion on the dial side of the plate to drive the motion wheels, which provide a 12:1 reduction from minutes to hours. Positioned on the back plate to control the hour striking is a count-wheel engraved with a seeded rose. The signature, *Eduardus East Londini*, is engraved in the lower part of the back plate.

Ilbert Collection
(Reg. CAI–2115)

Joseph Knibb

Table clock with quarter repeat
London, c.1675
Height 35 cm, width 24 cm, depth 15 cm

Joseph Knibb, the son of Thomas Knibb of Claydon in Oxfordshire, was born in 1640. Where he learned the art of clockmaking is unknown, but he is recorded working in Oxford; first in St Clements and then in Holywell Street. By January 1671 he had moved to London, where he established a business at 'The Dial' in Fleet Street and was enrolled as a Free Brother in the Clockmakers' Company. His was a prolific workshop producing clocks of high quality, and a good number of fine examples survive today. In 1697 Knibb retired to Hanslope in Buckinghamshire, where he died in 1711 at the age of seventy-one.

This small clock in a walnut case with gilt-brass mounts goes for eight days per winding and strikes a single blow on the larger bell at each hour. However, in addition to this rather simple striking system, the clock has a pull-quarter repeat mechanism of early design. On pulling a cord at the side of the case, a mechanism with cams mounted on the front plate causes two hammers to strike the last hour on the larger low bell, followed by the number of quarters past the hour on the smaller high bell: thus when the cord is pulled at 3.40 p.m., the clock will strike 'dong, dong, dong, ding, ding'.

In earlier clocks with count-wheel control, the count-wheel could not be used to repeat the striking because it always, in turning, moves forward to the next hour. In the mid-1670s a new striking mechanism called 'rack-and-snail' was introduced. It is attributed to Edward Barlow, a Catholic Priest from Charnock Richard in Lancashire, and its use was rapidly adopted in the majority of striking clocks. In this system, the positions of the striking levers and detents etc. are determined by a snailed cam on the hour wheel so that when the clock strikes, the rack-and-snail system returns the components to their original positions so that the striking can be repeated.

The dial of this clock is of simple, elegant design, with cherub-head spandrel mounts in the corners and a matted centre. There is floral engraving at the sides and the inscription, *Joseph Knibb London,* appears at the bottom. The chapter ring is relatively wide with bold roman hour numerals and a narrow minute circle numbered in arabic at five-minute intervals. The single winding hole shows it to be only a timepiece with no full striking. The movement is spring-driven with fusee, and has a verge escapement with a short bob pendulum. The back plate is beautifully engraved with flowers and foliage, and in a plain area bears the signature *Joseph Knibb Londini fecit.*

Ilbert Collection
(Reg. CAI–2143)

Pietro Tomasso Campani

Table night clock
Rome, 1683
Height 99 cm, width 57 cm, depth 28 cm

In the last quarter of the seventeenth century the popularity of the night clock was at its height, and nowhere more so than in Italy. In Rome the Campani family were the best-known makers. In 1655 Cardinal Farnese was ordered to provide a clock for Pope Alexander VII which would show the hours at night, but not in the traditional way that was simply by placing a candle in front of a standard table clock. Three brothers, Giuseppe, Pietro Tomasso and Matteo Campani from San Felice in Umbria, were working in Rome as clockmakers to the Pope, and they set about producing a clock to fit the bill.

Just a year later, in 1656, one of their clocks was presented to the Cardinal, and such was its success in achieving the goal imposed that the Campani brothers were granted a 'privilege' or patent which, although contested, remained with them. They then went on to make numerous examples of their new invention. As well as producing a clock with its own internal light source, they also invented a new form of silent escapement for particular use in night clocks so that the owner would not be kept awake by a ticking clock in the bedroom.

This particular clock is inscribed *Petrus Thomas Campanus Inventor Rome 1683*, and its case is typical of late seventeenth-century Italian work. It is veneered in ebony with elaborate gilt-brass mounts and inset with slabs of semiprecious stones. The columns are painted in imitation of blue marble and support a complex double pediment top. At the bottom there is a concealed drawer in which the winding key can be kept.

The dial is painted with depictions of the four ages of man, the four times of day and Chronos, beneath a semicircular aperture in which can be seen a revolving disc with two round holes diametrically opposite each other. Each of these holes reveals one of a series of hour numeral plates, odd numbers in one and even in the other. As the main disc revolves once in two hours, one of the two small apertures with the hour disc behind is visible in the semicircular opening. When one disc disappears out of view on the right-hand side, the next appears on the left with the appropriate numeral visible. The dial is also pierced around the top of the main aperture with quarters I, II, III and with the half-quarters as pierced inverted tear-drop holes. The oil lamp inside illuminates the revolving system so that the time can be seen in the dark, and there is a zinc-lined chimney which allows the heat and fumes to escape at the back.

The movement is ingenious in its method of achieving a silent operation but perhaps is not a step forward in terms of accurate timekeeping. A large spring drives the gear train of just three wheels, and the third wheel drives a pinion which is linked directly to the pendulum by a cranked lever mounted eccentrically on a disc. In order to carry the pendulum arrangement past its zero point, where it might have a tendency to stop at each revolution, there is a friction-tight fly in the form of a long bar with weights at each end. The rotation of this keeps the whole mechanism in constant motion and without any ticking sound.

Ilbert Collection
(Reg. CAI–2128)

Ahasuerus Fromanteel

Longcase clock
London, *c.1665*
Height 193 cm, width 30 cm, depth 20 cm

There is lately a way found out for making Clocks that go exact and keep equaller time than any now made without this regulator (examined and proved before his Highness the Lord Protector, by such doctors whose knowledge and learning is without exception) and are not subject to alter by change of weather, as others are, and may be made to go a week, or a month, or a year, with once winding up, as well as those that are wound up every day and keep time as well; and is very excellent for all House clocks that go either with springs or weights: and also Steeple clocks that are most subject to differ by change of weather. Made by Ahasuerus Fromanteel, who made the first that were in England: you may have them at his house on the bank side in Mosses Alley Southwark and at the sign of the Mermaid in Lothbury, near Bartholomew Lane end, London.

Ahasuerus Fromanteel's famous advertisement placed in the *London Mercury* in 1658 brings the clock-buying public's attention to the new technology that was the pendulum clock. Fromanteel had sent his son John to The Hague as part of his apprenticeship to learn the new technology from Salomon Coster who was making the new clocks for Christiaan Huygens. Fromanteel senior was born in Norwich in 1607 and apprenticed there to Jacques van Barton. He moved to London in 1631, became a Freeman of the Blacksmiths' Company and later in 1656 a Freeman of the Clockmakers' Company. On 3 September 1657 a contract was drawn up between Salomon Coster and Fromanteel's son John which was to last until May Day 1658. In the contract, John was to make clocks for which Coster would pay twenty gulden, unless Coster had provided the brass and steel, in which case he would be paid eighteen gulden. Coster would provide free beer, fire and light.

This new accuracy brought about a change in attitude to clocks. They were now commonly of eight-day duration and consequently of heavier construction: the driving weights alone could have a combined weight of 12.7 kg (28 lb). The need to protect the mechanism and dial of the clock from interfering hands and the need to support the increased weight of the clock led to the introduction of longcase or grandfather clocks, a style which was to remain popular for more than two centuries.

The clock has an ebonised pear-wood case of architectural style. Its dial shows hours and minutes and the clock strikes the hours using a count-wheel. The eight-day weight-driven movement has a verge escapement with a short 'bob' pendulum. Bolt-and-shutter maintaining power keeps the clock going during winding, an innovation introduced at this time to maintain the accuracy of the clock, and also to protect the escapement from damage during the winding process.

Fromanteel was one of the foremost makers of the new pendulum clocks in the 1660s, being one of those whose business in Southwark was not destroyed by the Great Fire in 1666. He also had a business in Amsterdam, where his family originated. He died in 1693.

Ilbert Collection
(Reg. CAI–2099)

Joseph Knibb

Longcase clock
London, *c.*1675
Height 195 cm, width 36.5 cm, depth 21 cm

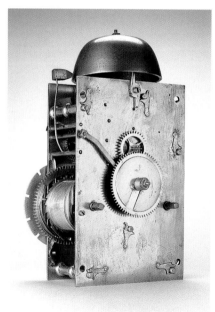

This clock by Joseph Knibb displays the next stage in the development of the longcase clock. Although its outward appearance is very similar to the Fromanteel clock described earlier, it is deceptive because this clock has an anchor escapement and a seconds-beating pendulum about one metre long, unlike the short bob pendulum on the Fromanteel clock. However, like the Fromanteel, this clock has bolt-and-shutter maintaining power and count-wheel striking.

The new anchor escapement appears in longcase clocks soon after 1670. Over the years there has been some debate concerning its inventor. It has been attributed to William Clement on the basis of a turret clock which he made for King's College, Cambridge, in 1671. Robert Hooke has also been credited with the invention of the escapement, based on a reference in William Dereham's *The Artificial Clockmaker* of 1696. Here Dereham states that to his knowledge Hooke had denied that Knibb had anything to do with it. Hooke, however, was not a clockmaker and there is no evidence to suggest that he ever worked on such an idea and, indeed, he never claimed it as his own.

The maker with the strongest claim to the invention of the new escapement has to be Joseph Knibb. Early in 1670 a clock with an anchor escapement was supplied to order to Wadham College, Oxford, a college which incidentally was close to the Knibb workshops in Holywell Street. Also in that same year, Joseph Knibb was charged with the job of converting the clock of St Mary the Virgin in Oxford to the new anchor escapement. While neither of these clocks provides proof that Knibb was the actual inventor of the escapement, the evidence seems to point strongly in his favour.

The escapement itself provided one significant advantage over its predecessor; the verge. The operating angle through which the pendulum needed to swing was reduced to an arc where the path of the circle and the cycloid are almost the same, thus reducing circular error to a minimum. An incidental advantage of the new escapement with its greatly-reduced operating arc was that it allowed for the introduction of the seconds-beating pendulum. This may seem on the surface to be a fairly trivial matter but it enabled the clockmaker to put seconds indication on the clock dial very simply – and seconds were by this time becoming a significant division of time, one in which those interested in accurate timekeeping had a serious interest.

Ilbert Collection
(Reg. CAI–2100)

Edward East

Longcase night clock
London, *c.*1685
Height 204 cm, width 44 cm, depth 24 cm

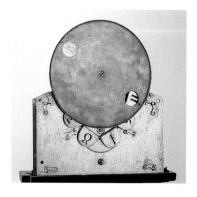

The popularity of ebonised architectural longcase clocks in London was short-lived. By the mid-1670s they were more commonly housed in cases of walnut, sometimes beautifully inlaid with marquetry designs, both geometric and pictorial, consisting of intricate inlays of coloured woods and ivory. The fashion for furniture decorated in this manner had come across the English Channel from the Netherlands, and it is not surprising to find that clock cases should be decorated en-suite to match side-tables and bureaux of similar style.

Such clocks were produced by nearly all the London makers and Edward East was no exception. This example by him has been recently restored and shows well the beautiful effect produced by using different colours to stain the woods and bone to produce inlays of flowers and birds. Many cases of this type unfortunately have stood for centuries in full sunlight and have no colour left, whereas here the original effect is still quite clear. The walnut panel for the door has ebony moulding around the outside and a lighter surround enclosing two panels of flowers. Similar decoration is used on the front of the plinth.

The hood, which lifts up to enable winding, has ebony twist pillars at the sides that twist in opposite directions and taper towards the top to provide an elegant frame for the dial, which is engraved all over with a fine design of flowers. In the upper part of the dial is a semicircular aperture that reveals a disc behind, in which are two holes. The holes each reveal a numeral pierced in a series of twelve plates, one for each hour. The chain and plates are carried round by a ten-sided wheel and the sequence of plates is arranged with every fifth plate anti-clockwise being the next number. As the wheel revolves, so each number is successively positioned behind the holes in the revolving disc to present itself through the aperture. The quarters are pierced I, II, and III in the fixed dial plate and the minutes are indicated by serrations in the upper edge of the aperture. At night an oil lamp inside the clock would be lit to illuminate the time through the numerals and pierced calibrations.

It is also worth noting that there is no striking mechanism in this clock: owners of a bedroom clock did not wish to be disturbed from their sleep by the loud clanging of a bell at every hour.

Purchased in 1980
(Reg. 1980,10–2.1)

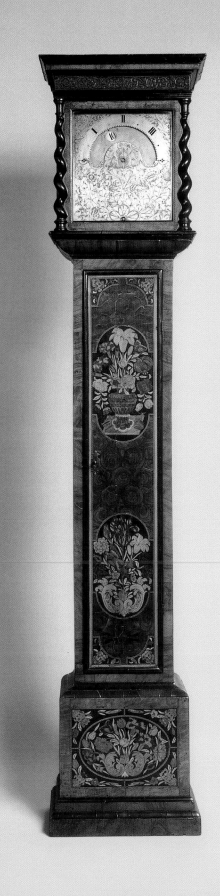

Thomas Tompion

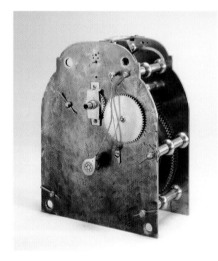

In 1674, a committee which included Christopher Wren, Robert Hooke and the astronomer John Flamsteed, set up by Charles II to investigate claims that variations in magnetic dip could be used to determine the longitude of a particular place, was asked to look into claims by a Frenchman, the Sieur de St Pierre. Through the king's mistress, Louise de Kéroualle, the Sieur had proposed to Charles II that longitude could be found by observing the motions of the moon. In response, Charles charged the committee to investigate the practicality of the Sieur's claim.

This led in 1675 to a Royal Warrant enabling an observatory, designed by Sir Christopher Wren, to be built at Greenwich, and for John Flamsteed to be the first Astronomer Royal. The Warrant began 'whereas we have appointed our trusty and well-beloved John Flamsteed, master of arts, our astronomical observer, forthwith to apply himself to the rectifying the tables of the motions of the heavens, and the places of the fixed stars, so as to find out the so-much desired longitude of places for the perfecting of the art of navigation'. Sir Jonas Moore supervised the construction of the building and commissioned two specially-designed regulators from the leading London clockmaker of the time, Thomas Tompion, and a third from a Lancashire clockmaker, Richard Townley, whose dead-beat escapement, subsequently modified by Tompion, was used in the clocks.

Thomas Tompion was baptised on the 25th of July, 1639, in Northill, Bedfordshire and lived in the nearby hamlet of Ickwell Green. Nothing is known of his early career. In 1671, he can be traced in London where he established a business in Water Lane just off Fleet street. In 1674, he supplied a turret clock for the Wardrobe Tower at the Tower of London and a quadrant for the Royal Society. The following year he made a watch for King Charles II. In 1675-6 he was commissioned to make the regulators for the new Greenwich Royal Observatory. Tompion became the most celebrated of all English clockmakers and established a business with a reputation second to none in Europe. He was admitted as a Free Brother in the Clockmakers' Company in 1671, was granted full freedom in 1647 and held the office of Master of the Company in 1703/4. He died in 1713 and was buried in Westminster Abbey.

Both of the Tompion clocks survive, one in the National Maritime Museum, the other in The British Museum, but the whereabouts of the Townley clock remain unknown. Astronomers had always been great campaigners for accurate clocks, essential to their work, and the clocks installed in the Greenwich Royal Observatory in 1676 were at the time the best in the world, enabling Flamsteed to record the motions of the planets and the moon and establish the true positions of the fixed stars.

The large square dials were velvet covered and while they seem at a glance to be of standard design, they are not so. The chapter ring is calibrated in hours I–XII, with an outer ring divided into minute divisions, all numbered and calibrated 1–60 twice, i.e. for a minute hand rotating once in two hours. The subsidiary dial above the centre is for seconds, divided to single seconds and also numbered 1–60 twice for a seconds hand revolving once every two minutes. Thus the time on the

TOP LEFT: Thomas Tompion
(Reg: CAI 2757)

TOP RIGHT: Royal Observatory, c.1680

ABOVE: John Flamsteed
(Reg: CAI 2725)

dial shown here is forty-four minutes past two o'clock and not twenty-two minutes past, as it first appears. However, this clock was designed specifically for use by an astronomer who was not concerned with the time of day. Above the VI numeral a silver plate around the winding hole is inscribed, *Sir Jonas Moore Caused this Movement With great Care to be thus made Ao 1676 by Tho Tompion*. At the top of the plate is the inscription *Motus Annus* indicating that the clock will run for a whole year on a single wind. Even so, the massive movement is furnished with maintaining power to keep the clock running during winding. Clearly these clocks were never meant to stop from one year to the next. When the clock was set up in Greenwich it had a two-seconds beating pendulum measuring 13 feet (3.96 m) long. After initial adjustments made to the escapement, Flamsteed recorded that the clocks were keeping time to within two seconds per day.

Following Flamsteed's death in 1719 his widow removed the clocks and instruments from the observatory on the grounds that they had been the property of her late husband. At some time after this, this clock was converted to domestic use by the replacement of the escape wheel so that it would function with a seconds pendulum. Recently, however, with funds provided by the Townley Group of The British Museum Friends, a new dead-beat pin-wheel escapement has been made by Jeremy Evans, curator at the Museum. The escapement is based on surviving sketches of Richard Townley's original concept and the clock now performs as it used to, with the pendulum beating two seconds and swinging at right angles to the dial.

Purchased in 1928
(Reg. 1928,6–7.1)

Thomas Tompion

Year-going table clock with quarter repeat, 'The Mostyn'
London, c.1690
Height 73.6 cm, width 34 cm, depth 24.5 cm

When it comes to opulence there are few, if any, English-made spring-driven clocks which would surpass this magnificent *tour de force* by Thomas Tompion. In the late seventeenth century, English weight-driven, year-going clocks were extremely rare, while spring-driven clocks of such long duration were non-existent. However, year-going spring clocks had been made in earlier times, and notable surviving examples are the silver-cased clock by Johann Sayler of Ulm made in about 1630 and the clock by Johannes Buschmann made in 1652 for Augustus, Duke of Braunschweig-Lüneburg-Wolfenbüttel. That is not to say that Tompion had any knowledge of these clocks.

Tompion's year-going clock marks the pinnacle of his achievement as a practical clockmaker. To make a clock that will perform efficiently for such a long period on a single wind is a most demanding challenge for even the most accomplished of makers. To increase the duration of clocks, extra wheels have to be added in the going train and this necessitates an increase in the strength of the mainspring. The result is that, if the proportions of the wheels and pinions are not of the most elegant, and if the forms of the teeth are anything but perfect, then the power needed to drive the machine becomes prohibitive. It comes as no surprise, therefore, that the making of such clocks was limited to a tiny number of craftsmen and that Thomas Tompion was the first in England to meet the challenge.

The year-duration going train consists of a fusee and great wheel which drives a six-wheel train terminating with a verge escapement of very small proportions, controlled by a short bob pendulum with spring suspension and a rise and fall mechanism.

The striking train is similarly extensive and here Tompion meets another daunting challenge. The striking train of an ordinary eight-day clock strikes 156 blows on the bell in a twenty-four-hour period or 1,092 blows in seven days. Tompion's year clock, therefore, has to strike the bell 56,940 times. In reality this clock runs for thirteen months and Tompion has even provided extra capacity so that the striking train can be used as part of the quarter-repeat system as well which means that the clock can actually strike over 60,000 times on a single wind.

The trains for the going and striking as far as the third wheels are mounted between massive lower plates, and the smaller and lighter components of the trains as well as the pull quarter-repeat mechanism are housed in the upper section. The pendulum swings in front of the movement and is regulated by a long blued-steel micrometer screw, turned by the capstan at its right-hand end. In the middle of the finely-matted dial centre, a sector aperture reveals a calendar giving the days of the week, each with a pictorial representation of its ruling deity.

The ebony-veneered oak case is lavishly decorated with silver and gilt-brass mounts of the highest quality. On the front of the domed top is a crowned shield bearing the royal arms. The clock is surmounted by the figure of Britannia holding a spear and a shield which bears the combined crosses of St George and St Andrew. The gilt-brass masks and the silver garlands around the base emphasize the superlative quality of the

mounts. This stupendous work by Tompion is thought to have been
made in the coronation year of William and Mary. The royal arms that
appear on the shield were used for only a few months during the summer of 1689 until the Scottish parliament agreed to recognize the joint
monarchy, at which time a different version combining the Stuart arms
with those of Nassau was used. The extremely high quality of all the
mounts on the clock and the engraving of the front plate of the movement have provoked suggestions that the work must have been done by
the best craftsmen of the time. The names Jean Berain and Jean Tijou
have both been suggested as contributors to this magnificent piece.

On the death of William III in 1702, the clock, which was kept in
the Royal Bedchamber, passed as a perquisite to Henry Sydney, Earl of
Romney, Gentleman of the Bedchamber and Groom of the Stole. Two
years later, when he died, it was left to the Earl of Leicester and then
passed by descent to Lord Mostyn, from whom it was purchased by
the Museum in 1982.

From 1793 the Mostyn family kept a written record of the clock's
performance over each year, noting the names of those present at the
annual winding ceremony. Although there are some gaps when the
clock lay dormant or the record was not made, it does give an interesting
insight into its performance. For instance, the record for 17 September
1884 reads: 'The clock was satisfactorily wound at 9.45pm by Robert
Walpole Esq., L.E. Bligh Esq. and Lord and Lady Mostyn for the first time
after their arrival at Mostyn Hall. It had not run down but had lost
2 hours'.

Purchased 1982
(Reg. 1982,7–2.1)

Thomas Tompion

Silver-gilt travelling clock
London, c.1700
Height 20 cm, width 11.5 cm, depth 8.5 cm

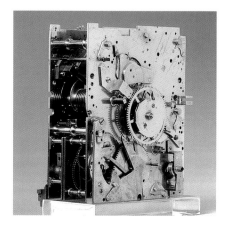

This clock by Thomas Tompion (1639–1713) is one of his most complicated. It has a pull-quarter repeat, an alarm and a grande-sonnerie striking mechanism. All this is squeezed into a very small space. Such was Tompion's ingenuity that he even housed the mainspring barrel for the striking mechanism inside the bell so that no available space was left unoccupied.

Originally the clock provided a complicated and rarely attempted refinement in the form of dual escapement control. This allowed the clock's owner to engage the pendulum whilst the clock was stationary and switch over to balance control when travelling. It is, however, a great pity that this mechanism was removed and replaced with a platform lever escapement, in the nineteenth century. Perhaps Tompion's original concepts were becoming troublesome and beyond the ability of its then repairer and its owner thought it better to butcher this rare clock in the name of reliable time-keeping rather than to preserve it for posterity.

The beautifully decorated silver champlevé dial has the usual hour numerals I–XII with lozenge half-hour marks within an outer circle for the minutes, with every fifth division numbered in Arabic. In the middle is an alarm-setting disc, which is rotated so that the required alarm time is beneath the pointed tail of the hour hand. In the corners are four key-operated subsidiary dials. The top two were used for regulation and are calibrated 0–60 and inscribed 'POVR REGLER LA PENDULE' to the left and 'POVR REGLER LE BALANCIER' to the right. The lower left dial is inscribed 'BALANCIER' and 'PENDVLE' and effects the change from one controller to the other, the lower right dial is inscribed 'SONNE SIL aux quart SILENCE' offering different striking options from complete grande-sonnerie to hours only or silence. The French inscriptions might suggest either a French patron or an English Huguenot customer, but certainly, he or she would have been a very wealthy person, for this clock would undoubtedly have been very expensive. The dial is signed on a scrolled label THO TOMPION LONDON. Unfortunately most of the under-dial mechanism is now missing.

It comes as no surprise that such an exquisite movement and dial is housed in a case of the finest quality. The frame of the case is of fire-gilded silver with inserted panels at the sides and back, cast and chased with foliage, grotesque figures, masks and cherubs. Even the carrying handle at the top is in the form of two addorsed caryatid figures. The designs used as the basis for the decoration of the clock are related to those of the Huguenot engraver and designer Daniel Marot, brought to London by William III.

Purchased in 1986
(Reg. 1986,3–6.1)

Thomas Tompion

Longcase clock, 'The Mulberry'
London, *c.*1701
Height 24.7 cm, width 49 cm, depth 23.5 cm

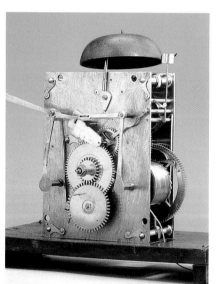

John Stalker and George Parker, *A Treatise of Japanning and Varnishing*, 1688:

> To stain a fine yellow – Take Burr or knotty Ash, or any other wood that is white, curled and knotty; smooth and rush it well, and having warmed it, with a brush dipt in Aqua fortis wash over the wood and hold it to the fire, as you do Japan-work until it leaves smoaking: when dry rush it again, for the Aqua fortis will make it very rough. If to these you add a polish, and varnish it with Seed-lacc, and then again polish it, you'l find no outlandish wood surpass it . . .

This month-going clock is housed in a beautiful 'mulberry-wood' case of the finest proportions, made using wood with extremely fine figures which create a superbly warm and sumptuous effect. The clock has been known for many years as 'The Mulberry Tompion' and was long thought to have been made from that wood. However, research shows that it is a burr wood, probably maple treated with nitric acid followed by linseed oil and lampblack to bring out the figures in the grain. That such a treatment was known at the turn of the eighteenth century is confirmed by Stalker and Parker's description of the process above.

The well-made, substantial movement has five pillars, but in contrast to Tompion's usual practice the plates are secured by pins rather than latches. The anchor escapement is controlled by a seconds-beating pendulum and the hour-striking mechanism has a count-wheel mounted on the outside of the back plate. There is also a bolt-and-shutter maintaining-power mechanism which keeps the clock going whilst it is being wound.

The immaculate dial has a finely matted centre with a chapter ring for hours and minutes and a subsidiary dial above the centre for seconds in the normal fashion. The movement is numbered 371 and a case has the number 19: by these numbers it can be dated to about 1701–02.

The case is of particularly fine proportions with a door at the front to allow access for winding. The hood is enhanced by plain columns with gilded-brass capitals and bases, and there are finely pierced fretwork panels which allow the sound of the bell to escape. To give the clock an even grander appearance there are five large gilded 'flaming vase' finials at the top. The overall effect of this most elegant of clocks with such a superb case is quite stunning and the fine proportions of the clock would have made it eminently suitable for a grandly furnished room in any stately house in England at the beginning of the eighteenth century. In 1701, such a clock would have cost about £20. In that year a bill to the Honourable Robert Harley Esq. from Thomas Tompion lists a 'month clock in an extraordinary case' at £17 10s.

Ilbert Collection
(Reg. CAI–2131)

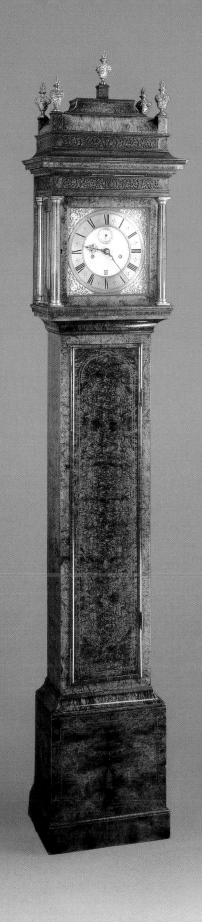

John Draper

Longcase clock
London, c.1705
Height 165 cm, width 51.5 cm, depth 27.5 cm

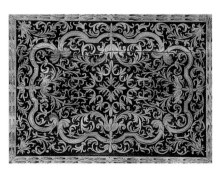

By 1700 the appearance of the London longcase clock had changed quite dramatically from the rather sombre look of the 1660s and the flamboyant era of floral marquetry designs of the 1670s and 1680s. By 1705 the proportions of the longcase clock had reached an elegance which would rarely be surpassed in the clocks that would follow in the coming century. By this time the scale and grandeur of English country houses had reached a new magnificence compared with their Tudor and Stuart predecessors. Larger rooms needed larger clocks and it comes as no surprise, therefore, to find much grander clocks becoming the fashion at the beginning of the eighteenth century. This clock by John Draper is over nine feet (2.75 m) tall, with a fine marquetry case of walnut inlaid with a most intricate pattern of darker woods in a design including foliate scrolls and birds. Another feature which becomes fashionable at this time is the glazed aperture, now commonly called a lenticle, which reveals the pendulum bob swinging behind it.

The hood is of the inverted bell design topped with three ball-and-eagle finials. In the early period, when longcase clocks were much smaller, the normal system was for the hood to be lifted by the owner in order to wind the clock. By 1700, however, clocks had generally grown in size to such an extent that lifting the hood was no longer a sensible means of access. It is therefore normal practice by this time for clocks to have both a hood which slides forward for removal and a hinged and locked front door to provide access for winding.

The dial is of absolutely standard design with finely-pierced hour and minute hands indicating against a silvered chapter ring and with a seconds dial below XII o'clock and a small date aperture above the VI numeral. The movement is also of standard design, going for eight days with an anchor escapement, seconds-beating pendulum and count-wheel striking.

Like many clockmakers working in London at the beginning of the eighteenth century, John Draper is relatively obscure. It is known, however, that he was apprenticed in the Clockmakers' Company in 1695 and gained his Freedom in 1703. The Company records show that he was still living in 1726 but nothing more is known of him. Another longcase clock bearing his name can be found in the Metropolitan Museum of Art in New York.

Presented by C. Sparkes in 1959
(Reg. 1959,2–2.1)

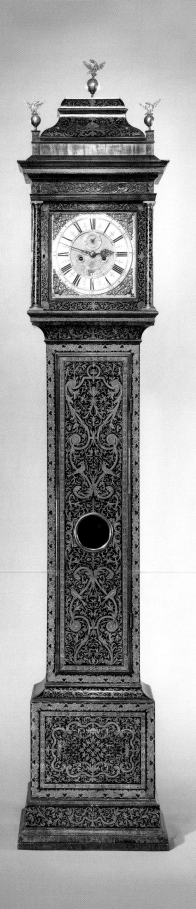

Daniel Quare

Year-going longcase clock
London, *c.*1710
Height 296 cm, width 66 cm, depth 38 cm

Standing at nearly ten feet high, this year-going longcase clock by Daniel Quare is of massive proportions and clearly destined for an impressive setting. The walnut case has plain columns with gilt-brass capitals and plinths and the top of the hood is domed in an inverted bell shape, topped by three large sphere and obelisk finials. The front door of the hood has a moulded gilt-brass bezel to retain the glass and the door is unusually enhanced with gilt-brass bands around the outside and with grotesque masks, foliage and strapwork mounts in the corners. Even the keyhole escutcheon is chased with a mask. The large rectangular base has brass scrolled feet and the lower front and side panels are overlaid with brass repoussé plaques, decorated with winged masks, strapwork, entwined snakes and swags of fruit.

The main dial is of standard design with subsidiary dials at the top; the left-hand dial showing the day of the week, the right-hand dial for rise-and-fall regulation. Apart from the size of the clock, perhaps the most interesting feature is the dial in the trunk door, which has the inscription, 'The long Hand is 365 Days in going Round and points the Days of the Months. The Hand with the Figure of the Sun shews how many Minuts (computed from the Cypher under 69) a true Sun Dial is Faster or Slower than this Clock, the Sun dayly varying from equal Time'. Thus, there are two hands on this dial, the longer of which makes one revolution in a year and indicates the month and date. The smaller hand moves back and forth through an arc of about 180 degrees to indicate the equation of time. Incorporated in the upper part of the main dial decoration is a shield with an unfinished and poorly engraved royal coat of arms, which has led some authorities to suggest that the clock has a royal provenance. It would seem more likely that these arms are a later attempt to enhance the clock's value, possibly as late as the early twentieth century.

Daniel Quare, a Quaker born in 1647, was admitted as a Free Brother in the Clockmakers' Company in 1671 and served as master in 1708. He later refused the office of Clockmaker to George I as his religion precluded him from swearing an oath of allegiance to the crown. His most famous surviving work takes the form of a gold pair-cased quarter-repeating watch made in 1687, now in the Ashmolean Museum collections. This watch is very likely the one which he submitted to James II and which gained the King's favour over a rival watch made by Thomas Tompion to Edward Barlow's design. Quare's clocks and watches are characterized by their high quality but, with the exception of his repeating mechanism for watches, he cannot be seen as an innovator. Quare continued in business on his own until about 1715 when he took Stephen Horseman into partnership. He died in Croydon in 1724 and was buried in Bunhill Fields in London. The business was then carried on by Horseman until bankruptcy befell him in 1733.

While the clock is signed on the dial, *Daniel Quare, London*, it is likely that the clock movement is the work of another hand. In *Philosophical Transactions of the Royal Society*, XXX (1720), there is a report of a letter in which Joseph Williamson asserted his right to 'the curious and useful

Invention of making clocks to keep time with the sun's apparent motion'. In the communication Williamson makes the following claim to the invention and making of clocks showing true solar time and points out that he made such clocks for Daniel Quare from about 1700 onwards. He said:

> And in the first place I must take notice of the Copy of a letter in this Book, wrote by one P. Kresa, a Jesuit, to me Mr Williamson,, Clockmaker to his Imperial Majesty: of a clock found in the late King Charles the Second of Spain's Cabinet, about the year 1699 or 1700 which sheweth both equal and apparent Time according to the Tables of Equation, and which went 400 days without winding up. This I am well satisfied is a clock of my own making; for about six years before that time, I made one for Mr Daniel Quare, for whom I then wrought mostly, which agrees with the Description that he gives of it, and went for 400 days. This clock Mr Daniel Quare sold, soon after it was made to go to the said King Charles the Second of Spain: and it was made so that if the Pendulum was adjusted to the sun's mean Motion, the Hands would show equal Time on two fixed Circles, on one the Hour, and the other the Minute . . . Soon after this clock was sent to Spain, I made others for Mr Quare which showed Apparent Time by lengthening and short-ening the Pendulum, in lifting it up and letting it down again, by a Rowler in the form of an ellipsis, through a slit in a piece of Brass, which the Spring at the Top of the Pendulum went through . . . For one of those, and not the first, made with the rising and setting of the Sun, Mr Quare sold to the late King William and it was set up at Hampton Court in his lifetime, where it hath been ever since . . . So that I think that I may justly claim the greatest right to this contrivance of making clocks to go with Apparent Time; and I have never heard of any such clock sold in England but was of my own making, though I have made them so long.

There seems to be no evidence to suggest that Quare refuted this assertion by Williamson, so we can only assume that he did indeed make equation clocks for Daniel Quare. Although this clock differs in its method of indication from those described by Williamson, it is nevertheless likely to be his work. This magnificent clock driven by a massive single weight also runs for a full year at one wind (400 days) and while the clock movement would have been made by Williamson, the case and the dial would have been the work of other skilled craftsmen employed by Quare.

Ilbert Collection
(Reg. CAI–2098)

Claude Duchesne

Quarter-chiming table clock
London, 1704
Height 51 cm, width 35.5 cm, depth 25 cm

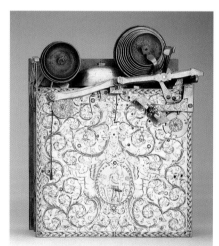

The Revocation of the Edict of Nantes by Louis XIV in 1685 caused a massive influx of Huguenot emigrants from France into England. As a religiously tolerant country, with pre-existing Huguenot communities, England was a natural sanctuary for those fleeing persecution in France. It is estimated that by 1700 the Huguenot population in the London area alone numbered between 20,000 and 25,000.

Claude Duchesne was one of those who left Paris to start a new life in London. He was made a Free Brother in the Clockmakers' Company in 1693 and lived in Long Acre in the parish of St Anne's, in Soho. There is also a recorded clock which is signed giving the address as 'Dean Street Soho'. Duchesne is thought to have lived until about 1730 and is known to have had at least one son, Antoine, who became a Freeman in the Goldsmiths' Company.

This austere ebony-veneered clock is not typical of the Huguenot style of 1700, when many clocks had either silver mounts or pierced gilt-metal single and double basket tops. Here the treatment is one of restraint, in a style which remained popular amongst English customers until well into the eighteenth century, with only the handle, four flame finials at the top and two vertical gilt-wood strips down the front and back doors.

The dial is less restrained, having a dial-plate finely engraved with a border of wheat ears enclosing arabesque foliate scrolls around the out-side of the chapter ring. There are four subsidiary dials and an aperture. Top left is a 'rise-and-fall' dial calibrated 5–60 for regulating the clock. In the upper right corner is a strike/silent dial. Bottom left is a month dial with the months named and depicted by their ruling planetary sign and with the number of days in the month. The bottom right-hand dial is engraved with the days of the week. In the middle, above the chapter ring, is a small rectangular aperture through which can be seen the date. Below this is an aperture revealing a small mock-pendulum, used to start the clock without the need to turn it round to gain access from the back. Finally, at the very bottom is a lever which activates shutters that cover the winding squares. The clock is signed on the dial *Claudius Du Chesne Londini Fecit* and inside the back plate is a faint, scratched inscription, *Le 13 May 1704 Claudius Duchesne Londini Fecit.*

The clock chimes the quarters on ten bells, has a pull-quarter repeat which sounds on four more bells and strikes the hours on a single low-pitched bell. The one-month, spring-driven movement has fusees and a verge escapement controlled by a pendulum. The movement back plate is even more sumptuously engraved than the dial, with copious foliate scrolling and two winged trumpeters flanking a central cartouche in which there is a depiction of *David with the Head of Goliath.*

Ilbert Collection
(Reg. CAI–2192)

Edward Cockey

Astronomical longcase clock
Warminster, Wilts., *c.*1720
Height 283 cm, width 73.5 cm, depth 39 cm

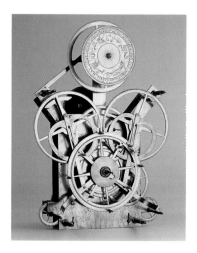

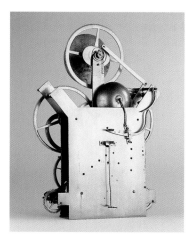

While it is true that the most successful and accomplished clockmakers tended to have their businesses in London, there were always talented makers to be found further afield. One of these was Edward Cockey of Warminster in Wiltshire (1669–1768), a maker best known for a series of massive astronomical clocks which he made at the beginning of the eighteenth century. Generally standing more than ten feet high, they would have been suitable only for the most cavernous of entrance halls or chambers. One is known to have been made for Thomas Thynne, Viscount Weymouth at Longleat, where it survives to this day. Another is thought to have been presented to Queen Anne. Yet another is in The British Museum, and while most of them are in their original cases (uniquely in the form of a Corinthian half-column), the museum's example is now in a custom-made mahogany case made in about 1760.

The complex dial is in the form of an extraordinarily-detailed calendar. The main dial has a central rotating disc showing the moon's age, one to twenty-nine-and-a-half days, with the phase of the moon indicated by a revolving spherical moon. There is also a scale with a short gilt pointer to show the sun's position in the zodiac. To each side of the central dial are moving shutters, which by their position show the times of sunrise and sunset throughout the year. The main chapter ring is marked I–XXIV and has a minute hand which revolves once in two hours. Outside the chapter ring is a rotating ring with an applied gilt sunburst on a painted blue sky to show the hours of the day against the main chapter ring. Within this main chapter ring is the maker's name and two smaller, silvered shutters at the end of a narrow dark blue sector aperture. When the sun effigy disappears behind the main night shutters, a small disc engraved with a starburst appears in the small aperture to show the night hours against the smaller chapters IIII-XII-VIII. When the night is over, the star disappears behind the left-hand silver shutter and the main sun-effigy appears from behind the large left-hand night shutter. As the seasons change so the dark-blue night shutters and the silvered day shutters move to show the true length of the day and night.

In the arch above the main dial, a scale at the top shows the equation of time. An upper aperture shows the month, the date and the sign of the zodiac. The central aperture reveals a revolving disc engraved with the Sundays in the liturgical calendar, while the lower aperture shows the days of the week, each with its ruling planet. The small dial to the right shows the date and that on the left has a hand for regulating the clock.

An intriguing feature of this clock is the heraldic lion crest that sits in the break-arch of the hood. Sitting on a twisted *torse*, or wreath, is a gilt lion in the *sejant guardant* position. This was probably transferred from the original case. Unfortunately, a number of different families used this form of crest in their armorial bearings, making it impossible to be specific about its ownership.

Ilbert Collection
(Ref. CAI–2124)

George Graham

Quarter-repeating table clock
London, *c.*1730
Height 37 cm, width 21.5 cm, depth 15 cm

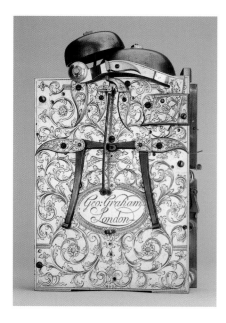

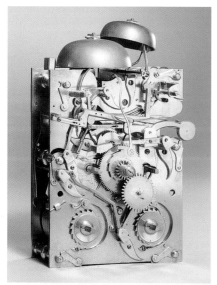

George Graham, born either at Horsegills, Kirklington or at Fordlands in Irthlington, Cumberland in about 1673, was apprenticed to Henry Aske in London in 1688. He became a Freeman in the Clockmakers' Company in 1695 and worked for the celebrated maker Thomas Tompion. By 1711 Graham had clearly shown his ability and worth to his employer because, having married Tompion's niece Elizabeth in 1704, he was taken into partnership and ran the business until Tompion's death in 1713. Graham continued the business after Tompion's death and himself became Master of the Clockmakers' Company in 1722. He died in 1751, having trained a number of apprentices, one of whom was Thomas Mudge, and was buried with Tompion in Westminster Abbey.

Graham's Fellowship of the Royal Society in 1720 was to some extent central to the improvements in horology which took place in the first half of the eighteenth century. A maker of some of the finest clocks of his generation, he was also a pioneer in the making of instruments for astronomical observation. He had studied astronomy himself, gave papers on the subject to the Royal Society, and his instrument making skills were second to none. In 1725 he supplied an eight-foot radius mural quadrant, mounted on a frame made by Jeremiah Sisson, to Edmund Halley at the Greenwich Observatory where it was to remain in use until 1750. Indeed, such was the esteem in which this instrument was held that it merited a whole chapter in Robert Smith's standard work, *A Compleat system of opticks* published in 1738. Graham's other instruments include a transit instrument and a zenith sector for Halley's successor, James Bradley.

This example of Graham's work is a small ebony-veneered spring-driven table clock with pull-quarter repeat on two bells, numbered 689 in the clock series begun by Tompion and continued by Graham. If anything, the clock is rather old-fashioned in appearance but this style of clock did continue in English clockmaking until the end of the eighteenth century, so it must be assumed that there was a market for such restrained designs, albeit with rather fine silver spandrels at the dial corners. The two subsidiary dials at the top are for strike/silent on the right and regulation on the left.

One unique feature of this clock is the maintaining power system. Here, the maintaining power is activated by a lever which, in turn, is operated by the chamfered winding key as it is pushed onto the winding square.

Ilbert Collection
(Reg. CAI–2116)

RIGHT: George Graham

Henry Bridges

Monumental astronomical clock, 'The Microcosm'
Waltham Abbey, c.1733
Dial and movement: height 77 cm, width 38 cm, depth 13 cm

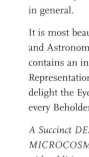

In Justice to the Memory of the late Mr. Henry Bridges of Waltham Abbey, Architect, I must inform the Reader, that the MICROCOSM was constructed by that excellent Artist. It was the Produce of more than twenty Years close Study and Application; and when completed, it received the Approbation of the Nobility, the Royal Society, the Gentry, and the curious Part of Mankind in general.

It is most beautifully compos'd of Architecture, Sculpture, Painting, Music, and Astronomy, according to the most approved Rules and Principles; and contains an infinite Variety of Moving Figures, whose Motions are a judicious Representation of Life. The Beauties of its internal Parts are calculated to delight the Eye, please the Ear, and improve the Mind; its external to strike every Beholder with Admiration and Magnificence of its Structure.

A Succinct DESCRIPTION OF THAT Elaborate PILE OF ART, called the MICROCOSM With a Short Account of the SOLAR SYSTEM, third edition with additions, Coventry, MDCCLXIII

The clock consisted of a large edifice in the form of a Roman temple, ten feet high and six feet wide (305 x 183 cm). A number of levels displayed representations of the nine Muses on Parnassus, Orpheus charming the wild beasts in the forest, a grove with birds flying and singing, a clock with both the Ptolemaic and Copernican celestial systems and a landscape with a prospect of the Ocean and ships sailing. The foreground was animated with coaches, carts, chaises, people, birds and dogs. Finally, there was a busy carpenter's yard. An organ, harpsichord, spinet, flute and whistle with thoroughbass accompaniment played eight melodies:

At length all the various Parts of this Machine are at once presented to the Spectator's View in Motion, when upwards of one thousand two Hundred Wheels and Pinions move all together; And during the whole Performance, it plays several fine Pieces of Music on the Organ, in a very elegant Manner; and the Organ is likewise provided with a Set of Keys, so that Ladies or Gentlemen may, themselves perform on the Organ what Pieces of Music they best like.

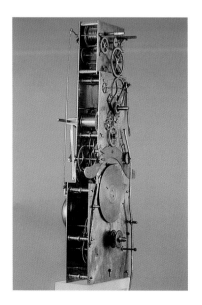

This monumental clockwork automaton was conceived as an entertainment. Thanks to researches into advertisements for the 'The Microcosm' by a number of people, particularly John R. Milburn and W.R. and V.B. McLeod, it is known that the edifice was exhibited in London and various locations around the country, in America, in Ireland and even in Jamaica. Following the death of Henry Bridges in 1754 'The Microcosm' continued to travel, but at some time must have fallen into dereliction and disrepair. There is even a tradition that it was destroyed during the French Revolution. It was rediscovered in Paris in 1938 by C.A. Ilbert, but sadly only the clock dial and movement had survived and, indeed, an extra quarter-striking train had been added to the mechanism.

Ilbert Collection
(Reg. CAI–2101)

John Naylor

Astronomical clock
Nantwich and London, *c.*1725
Height 84 cm, width 57.5 cm, depth 29.5 cm

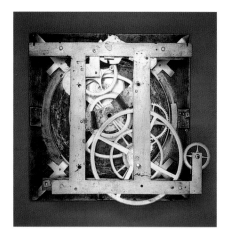

The eighteenth century saw a resurgence in the fashion for clocks specially designed for owners who had an interest in all things astronomical. Clearly, the more impressive and complex the dial indications were, the more opportunity was afforded the owner to demonstrate his knowledge of the universe to his peers. Such clocks were not a new idea but had their origins as far back as the medieval period, when public clocks such as those in Strasbourg Cathedral or in the Old Town Square in Prague were intended to demonstrate the wonders of God's universe to the common people. In the sixteenth century a similar fashion existed in the princely *Kunstkammer*, where astronomical clocks on a grand scale by such eminent makers as Eberhard Baldewein and Jost Bürgi were clearly made to impress.

John Naylor came from Nantwich in Cheshire but very little is known of him beyond the existence of a small number of clocks; in particular two magnificent astronomical clocks, one in The British Museum collections and the other in Paris in the Musée des Arts et Métiers. Apart from the clock itself, there is also a large print published in 1726, intended to show the intricacies of the dial. An interesting alteration to the print has been made to accommodate the new Gregorian calendar adopted in England in 1752.

The large case is typically English, in ebony-veneered oak and with very little decoration. It does, however, have a turntable base to allow the clock to be rotated for winding and for access to the back without turning the whole clock – something of a necessity in such a large and heavy clock. The conventional eight-day movement has fusees and verge excapement with spring-suspended pendulum, but the complicated under-dial work is far from standard. One interesting feature is the support for the pendulum, which is a high-arched steel hoop designed to raise the pendulum in order to accommodate it within the case. The movement back plate is engraved with a fine border of wheat ears enclosing foliate scroll decoration with birds and a mask in the centre. The blued-steel hands are pierced and indicate against the inner ring with its unusual wavy hour numerals. The fixed outer ring is calibrated for minutes.

In the arch is a finely-engraved depiction of Apollo the sun-god in his chariot, crossing the sky, with the lion of the constellation of Leo in the background. Around the outside, in the spaces between the dials and the main chapter ring, are beautifully-executed depictions of the four elements: earth, air, fire and water. Two subsidiary dials at the top, one in the lower left corner and a small one on the central vertical bar, are set manually to give information relating to the solar and lunar cycles, to enable the two pointers to the left of the main chapter ring to be set to show the date of Easter in both Julian and Gregorian terms against the wide calendar ring. This calendar, engraved with saints' days, revolves once per year around the fixed minute ring. Joining the minute ring to the central hour ring are two curved horizons which pass over a celestial ring engraved with the constellations of the zodiac between the two tropics. This planispheric map of the heavens rotates once in a sidereal

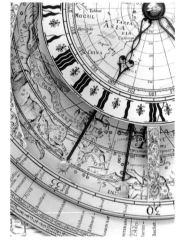

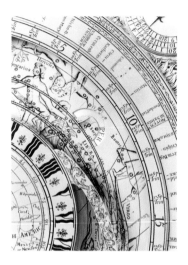

year (366 sidereal days, equivalent to 365 solar days). Moving over the celestial ring are sun and moon effigies which rotate once per day to show their times of rising and setting as they pass between the horizons, and also to show their positions in the zodiac throughout the year. In addition to this, a small semicircular aperture in the celestial ring gives the moon's apogees and perigees, the points at which the moon is furthest from or nearest to the earth. The fixed chapter ring, engraved with the hours, encloses a terrestrial planisphere centred on the north pole. Between the hour numerals XII and III and the map is a scale that shows the time of high tide at London Bridge.

Purchased in 1985
(Reg. 1985,10–5.1)

AN
EXPLANATION
OF AN
Astronomical Clock,
THE WORKMANSHIP OF
Jos. NAYLOR, Joyner;
Near *Namptwich* in *Chefhire*,

Is to be disposed of by One hundred Chances, at Two Guineas each, which are to be decided by a Machine;

CONSISTING
Of Two Wheels running reverse to each other, whose quick Motion shall suddenly stop of itself, and the Ticket numbered with the same, that appears on the Two Wheels, when the Machine stops,

Is entitled to the

CLOCK;

And the TICKET that answers to the Number on the Two Wheels, that is next under the winning Number,

Is entitled to the

DECIDING MACHINE.

The Clock will be fixed at a convenient Apartment near *St. James's*, whereof Notice shall be given, and the winning Chance decided April, 1751.

George Lindsay

Organ clock
London, *c.*1760
Height 91.5 cm, width 51 cm, depth 37 cm

Geo. Lindsay, Servant to the Prince of Wales. This is the original inscription on this magnificent organ clock by George Lindsay, but it was covered over by a signature plaque which reads, *Geo. Lindsay Watch maker to his Majesty.*

A Royal Warrant was issued to George Lindsay on 12 December 1760, appointing him as 'Watchmaker in Ordinary', an office he held until his death in 1776. A privileged office of this kind was often used in advertising, so it comes as no surprise to find watch-papers inscribed *G. Lindsay, watch maker to His Majesty and Her Royal Highness the Princess Dowager of Wales.* Lindsay is known to have been working from about 1743 and had his business at 'The Dial' in the Strand, London. Just a small number of pieces are known to survive from his workshop including a longcase clock formerly in the Wetherfield Collection, a watch in the Clockmakers' Company collections and this splendid organ clock. The clock can be dated from the plaque added following Lindsay's appointment as Royal watchmaker in 1760.

This mahogany-cased clock, standing more than three feet high, has gilt-brass columns at the corners and a gilt-brass base with large scroll feet. The top of the case is in the form of a miniature pipe organ, although the pipes are simply decorative. Sixteen square-section wooden pipes are situated in the back above the bellows and wind chest and there are two manual stops which allow the pipes' register to be changed from four feet to two feet as required.

Inside the case is a large horizontally-mounted, pinned and hooped barrel which 'plays' eight tunes on the organ – 'Julien's Polka', 'Swiss Waltz', 'Hart's Quadrille', 'Danwoius Quadrille', 'Swiss Gallopade', 'Cacoucha Dance', 'Redowa Polka' and 'Krakoviak Dance'. Sadly, the clock no longer plays these eighteenth century melodies, the music barrel having been re-pinned in the nineteenth century to play completely different music, including a piece from Weber's 'Der Freischütz' of 1821.

Around the main chapter ring, in addition to the tune title ring, there is a rise-and-fall dial calibrated 5–60 to the upper right, which raises or lowers the pendulum to finely adjust the rate of the clock from the front, a GOING/STOPT dial to the left which locks the pendulum when the clock is moved, a STRIKE/SILENT dial which silences the striking of the hours and a PLAY/NOT PLAY which silences the music that otherwise would play at three-hourly intervals, or at will by pulling a cord. Each tune is played three times before the clock automatically switches to the next one.

The timekeeping element of the clock is of standard form with fusees for both going and hour striking trains and it has a verge escapement controlled by a pendulum with an aperture in the dial for the false pendulum, used to start the clock without having to turn it around.

Ilbert Collection
(Reg. CAI–2135)

Henry Jenkins

Astronomical clock
London, 1778
Height 67 cm (without plinth), width 61 cm, depth 46 cm

In the second half of the eighteenth century interest in astronomy was perhaps at its height. The two transits of Venus in 1761 and 1769 had been earnestly followed by such august bodies as the Royal Society, and the work of astronomers such as James Ferguson had done much to popularize the subject among the large fraternity of gentlemen scientists. Astronomical clocks were understandably popular.

Henry Jenkins was born and educated in Cornwall. At the age of ten he was apprenticed as a tailor, but he also acquired knowledge of clockmaking and astronomy. He first appears in London in about 1755 and in the following five years made at least four clocks of increasing complexity. In 1778 he published a small treatise entitled *A Description of Several Astronomical and Geographical Clocks*. In the second edition of the treatise Jenkins described in some detail this particular clock, which he judged his most complicated. The illustration from the treatise (bottom) shows the original design of the case.

The clock has astronomical indications on two large dials. The upper dial is in the form of an orrery with the six known planets, Mercury, Venus, Earth, Mars, Jupiter and Saturn, revolving around a fixed sun. It is possible that the Jupiter gearing, which provides an orbit of 4334.3 days, may be Jenkins's more accurate contribution (it is now calculated at 4332.595 days).

The lower dial has a series of subsidiaries arranged around it. The large subsidiary dial at the top shows hours, minutes and centre-seconds. The smaller subsidiaries are a calendar to the left and a dial showing the time of high tide at various ports to the right. The main dial consists of a planisphere showing the positions of the sun, moon and the earth relative to the stars. The central, silvered disc is a plane projection of the heavens centred on the celestial north pole and revolving once in a sidereal year. It is engraved with all the major stars known at the time, with concentric circles for the equator and the two tropics, and the eccentric circle of the ecliptic.

The movement of the clock is equally impressive, with a back plate engraved with the chinoiserie designs commonly found on clock plates in the third quarter of the eighteenth century. It is designed to go for eight days and is controlled by a pendulum. The clock also plays music: one of the tunes, entitled 'Air by Mudge', written by Richard Mudge (brother of the famous clockmaker), is not known by musicologists to exist in any other form.

Purchased in 1992
(Reg. 1992,10–1.1)

George Graham

Longcase precision regulator with equation of time indicator
London, c.1745
Height 230 cm, width 48 cm, depth 26 cm

By the early years of the eighteenth century it was realized that tempera-ture change was the enemy of accurate timekeeping. In any pendulum clock, in general terms, it is the length of the pendulum that determines the rate at which it swings. This in turn controls the rate at which the clock runs and thus its accuracy. It is not helpful, therefore, that a pendu-lum gets longer when heated and shorter when cooled. George Graham, a Fellow of the Royal Society and one of the leading clock-, watch- and instrument-makers in eighteenth century London, was the first success-fully to apply temperature compensation to a pendulum clock in the form that it appears in this example of his work. In 1726 he published a paper entitled, 'A contrivance to avoid irregularities in a clock's motion' in *Philosophical Transactions of the Royal Society*, in which he says that in about 1715 he tried to see whether there was any considerable difference in the expansion of different metals when subjected to temperature change. The result of his investigations was the mercury pendulum.

Here, the brass pendulum rod carries a glass jar containing mercury so that, as the brass rod expands and contracts, the mercury expands and contracts in the opposite direction, in order to keep the effective length of the pendulum constant. This weight-driven, month-going longcase regu-lator has Graham's dead-beat escapement, an innovation he invented in about 1719, which also improved the accuracy of clocks, and bolt-and-shutter maintaining power.

Following the invention of the pendulum in 1657, clocks became sufficiently accurate to need a table showing the difference between the time shown by a sundial and that shown by a mean-time clock through-out the year. In practice this difference, known as the equation of time, means that the clock and the sundial or solar observation will only be the same on four occasions in the year. The problem is caused by the fact that the earth's orbit around the sun is elliptical rather than circular and that the earth's axis is tilted in relation to the celestial equator. The added sophistications on this clock are the secondary gilt minute hand which shows true solar minutes (sundial time) and the dial in the arch which, as well as being a calendar, shows the equation of time in minutes and seconds for each day of the year. With all these sophistications, this regu-lator represents the highest degree of accuracy available at the time and, being made by one of the most celebrated makers, would have been a highly-prized possession.

Formerly in the Ilbert Collection
(Reg. CAI–2132)

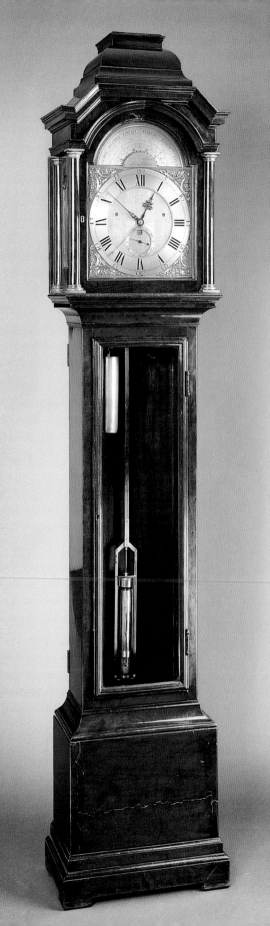

John Ellicott

Portable observatory regulator
London, c.1765
Height 173 cm, width 43.5 cm, depth 19.5 cm

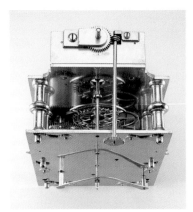

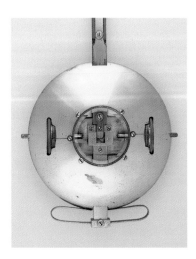

In the mid-eighteenth century astronomers, Royal Society Fellows and gentlemen scientists anticipated with excitement the prospect of an astronomical event which happened only rarely: the transit of Venus, in which the planet Venus would pass across the face of the sun. The astronomer Edmund Halley (1656–1742) had predicted that transits would occur in 1761 and 1769. Though he knew he would not live to see the event, he urged those who would to make every effort to record the fullest details. The data gained would enable astronomers to calculate the true distance between the earth and the sun. To achieve this, readings from a number of different locations around the globe would be necessary. Essential for the observations were a first-class regulator, a telescope fitted with a micrometer and a tent to protect these instruments from inclement weather.

The Royal Society organised voyages to observe the transits, and for these regulators such as this example by the firm of Ellicott of 17 Sweetings Alley, Royal Exchange, were specifically made. There is no evidence to connect this particular clock with the transit voyages, but it is certainly of the period and was designed to be portable. It could equally have been used on any one of a number of voyages of exploration, as such regulators were essential for establishing the longitude of a particular place as a base for surveying.

The regulator has a plain, solid mahogany case, which formerly had clamps to hold the pendulum when it was being transported. In more recent times, the plain top of the case has been modified into an arched top with acrotier decorations at the corners. This finely-made precision regulator has a substantial month-going movement with a Graham dead-beat escapement. The temperature compensation pendulum designed by Ellicott himself was first announced to the Royal Society in his 1752 paper 'A Description of Two Methods, by which the Irregularity of the Motion of a Clock, arising from the influence of Heat and Cold upon the Rod of the Pendulum, may be prevented'. In it Ellicott said that he first came to consider this form of pendulum in 1732 and placed designs for such a device in the hands of the Royal Society in 1738.

The dial is laid out in typical regulator style, with an outer circle of minutes numbered at five-minute intervals, a subsidiary dial of seconds and with the less important hours visible through an aperture below the centre. A subsidiary dial in the arch has a small hand used for precise regulation. Ellicott's pendulum relies on the differential expansion of the brass and steel in the composite pendulum rod acting on pivoted levers within the bob, causing it to rise or fall with an increase or decrease in temperature.

Lent by the School of Oriental and African Studies, London

Thomas Mudge

Lever clock
London, c.1754
Height 30.5 cm, width 23.5 cm, depth 14.8 cm

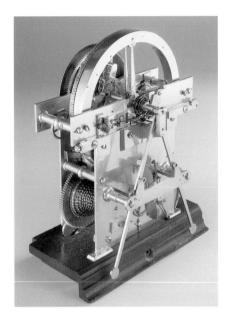

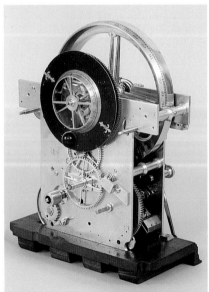

One of the most important clocks made by Thomas Mudge is this innocent-looking table clock finished in about 1754. The clock, now known as 'Mudge's Experimental Lever clock', contains the first example of his detached lever escapement; a major technological advance for portable timekeepers which, in a modified form, became a standard for watches and is still used today.

The main dial shows hours, minutes and seconds and there are lunar indications in the arch. The escapement is controlled by a large oscillating balance, mounted in the same plane as the plates of the clock on a balance staff running in anti-friction rollers with counterbalances – seemingly a direct follow-on from John Harrison's ideas. There are also brass and steel bimetallic compensation curbs to counteract the effects of temperature change. The escapement is driven by a mechanism known as a remontoire, in which a small spring, used to power the escapement and keep the balance oscillating, is rewound periodically by the main driving spring, in this case every twelve-and-a-half minutes. The purpose of this is to reduce the errors in timekeeping caused by differences in the power of the mainspring. Thus, instead of the errors being large and affecting the whole running period, they are reduced and averaged over a repeated twelve-and-a-half minute period.

The clock also has an extremely accurate lunar train, using under-dial epicyclic gears to achieve a lunar indication with an error of only one fifth of a second per twenty-nine-and-a-half-day lunation. It is tempting to suggest that this clock was intended as an entrant for a prize under the terms of the Longitude Act, but there is no evidence to show that Mudge ever submitted it to the Board of Longitude for consideration. In contrast to some of the other characters who appear in the longitude story, Mudge was clearly a self-effacing man who did not covet the recognition so hotly pursued by others. In a letter to his patron Count Maurice von Brühl, concerning the invention of the lever escapement, he wrote in August 1766, 'it [the escapement] has great merit and will, in a pocket watch particularly, answer the purpose of time-keeping better than any there at present known'. He did not, however, guard his invention with patents or documents deposited at the Royal Society. Indeed, ten years later in another letter to von Brühl, he wrote 'as to the honour of the invention, I must confess, I am not at all solicitous about it: whoever would rob me of the honour'.

The clock has an illustrious history, having been owned by the engineer, Isambard Kingdom Brunel (1806–1859). It was later acquired by the horological collector Courtenay Adrian Ilbert and came to the Museum in 1958.

Ilbert Collection
(Reg. CAI–2118)

RIGHT: Thomas Mudge (Reg: 1995,9-7.1)

Thomas Mudge

Travelling clock
London, c.1768
Carrying case: height 10 cm, width 18 cm, depth 15 cm. Clock case: diameter 15.2 cm

Following his experimental clock of c.1754 in which he incorporated his first lever escapement (see page 118), Thomas Mudge went on to make only a small number of timepieces incorporating the new escapement. The best-known of these, the watch made for Queen Charlotte in 1769, is still in the Royal Collections.

This little travelling clock is thought to be the second of Mudge's clocks to contain his new lever escapement. It is without doubt a *tour de force* of the clockmaker's art and typical of his work. This marvellous eight-day clock strikes the hours and sounds the last hour and quarter at the pull of a cord. The movement is a highly complex arrangement of gear trains and striking mechanisms, all arranged in a full-plate construction, making it an extremely demanding piece to work with. The lever escapement is mounted on a platform at the top of the clock and is displayed beneath a round glazed panel in the top of the case. The hours and quarters are struck on two bells mounted on the back plate.

The dial is of the highest quality in white enamel with arabic minutes, roman hours and a subsidiary dial at XII o'clock for seconds, numbered every fifth second 5–60. The gold hands for hours and minutes are very finely finished and the seconds are shown by a slender blued-steel hand. In the lower centre the makers' name is simply inscribed in capitals, THO MUDGE LONDON. The movement and dial are housed in an unusual cylindrical tortoiseshell-veneered case with gilt-brass bezel and ball feet, and there is also a mahogany carrying-case for protection during transport.

The clock was originally made for a Mr Geddes and work began on it in about 1766. By 1774, however, it had been purchased by Mudge's patron Count von Brühl, in whose family it remained by descent until it was purchased by The British Museum. In correspondence with von Brühl, Mudge referred to this clock as the 'little clock'. In 1774 he wrote, 'I am glad that you have got the little clock that was Mr Geddes''. The clock was then improved by Mudge and by 1777 he was clearly happy with its performance, saying to von Brühl, 'I am highly pleased with the going of your little clock, it is certainly greatly beyond what I expected from it, as the mode of executing the balance work is not so clever as it might have been, if going well had been the only consideration'. Here he refers to the fact that the clock has striking and repeating work and is not a simple timepiece.

Purchased in 1995
(Reg. 1995,2–7.1)

RIGHT: Count Maurice von Brühl (CAI-2710)

John De Lafons

Regulator
Royal Exchange, London, 1780
Height 201 cm, width 48.5 cm, depth 25.5 cm

The sidereal day is marked by the successive passing of the fixed stars and is shorter than the twenty-four-hour, mean solar day. This phenomenon results from the fact that the earth follows the path of its orbit and in consequence has to turn slightly further round to present the same aspect to the sun each day. This does not happen with much more distant fixed stars. The sun passes overhead 365 times in a solar year but the fixed stars pass overhead 366 times in the same period, a difference of one day per year, or three minutes and fifty-six-and-a-half seconds per day.

Observatory regulators showing sidereal time were commonly used by astronomers in their observations. It is therefore not surprising that clocks which indicate sidereal time were popular with amateur astronomers and gentlemen of science in an age when all matters scientific fascinated.

George Margetts of Cheapside, London (1748–1808) is best known for his astronomical watches and a small group of regulators which indicate both mean solar time and sidereal time on a single dial. When this clock, signed *John De Lafons Royal Exchange London*, is compared with those by Margetts there is virtually no difference between them. De Lafons had his business at 66 Threadneedle Street in London between 1793 and 1816, initially working on his own but later in partnership with his son Henry. In 1801, he received an award of thirty guineas from the Royal Society of Arts for a remontoire mechanism, and in 1805 was granted a patent for a marine chronometer with an alarm. The similarity between the series of Margetts regulators and the example by De Lafons suggests that they were all made by the same maker, probably Margetts, but possibly De Lafons or, indeed, an unknown trade maker who was supplier to them both. In this context, it is most interesting that an original signature on the dial of this clock has been punched out from behind, before that of De Lafons was engraved.

The regulator is month-going and housed in a finely-made mahogany case with raised panels at the sides of the hood and on the plinth. The movement is mounted on a massive cast iron frame attached to the very substantial back-board of the case. The dead-beat escapement has a steel escape wheel and jewelled pallets and is controlled by a grid-iron pendulum. The quality of the wheel-work is exceptional. The whole movement is built upside-down with the escapement at the bottom. The geared conversion from mean solar time to sidereal time is so accurate that the theoretical error is only two seconds per year.

The two times are shown on a composite dial with an outer ring for sidereal minutes and three subsidiary rings down the middle with sidereal hours, minutes and seconds at the top, middle and bottom respectively. Each of these rings has within it a rotating disc which shows the mean solar equivalent.

Bequeathed by Miss Diana Walker in 1998
(Reg. 1998,7–4.1)

Thomas Earnshaw/
Joseph Catherwood

Longcase regulator
London, *c.1795*
Height 208 cm, width 51 cm, depth 27.5 cm

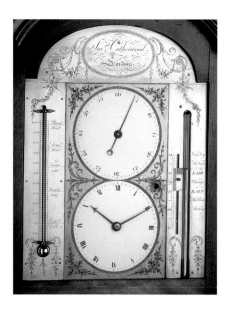

From the middle years of the eighteenth century, in the age of Enlightenment, and perhaps inspired by the two transits of Venus in 1761 and 1769, a number of private observatories were set up in Britain. A particularly famous one was that which King George III had built at Kew, where he personally tested John Harrison's timekeeper H5. Less well-known was the astronomer William Larkins, whose private observatory was at Blackheath, London. For his observations Larkins would have needed a good quality telescope and a high-quality regulator to provide accurate timekeeping.

It is highly likely that this superb regulator was the one which Larkins used. There is no absolute proof of such a provenance, but the sale catalogue of 23 June 1800 listing the contents of Larkins' observatory describes 'an excellent transit clock, compound pendulum, barometer and thermometer within, in a handsome mahogany case, Earnshaw.' The name Earnshaw in connection with this clock is a perfectly logical one, for while it is signed Catherwood, the whole design of the movement and case point to Thomas Earnshaw as the maker rather than Joseph Catherwood, who is not known to have been anything more than a retailer. Compelling evidence for an early change in the name on the clock is that the dial was punched out from the back to remove an original name before Catherwood's name was added. The original name cannot now be discerned. Further evidence exists from Earnshaw himself in his 1808 publication *Longitude. An Appeal to the Public*, where he says, 'The best clock I ever made, was for Mr. Larkins of Blackheath'. It is very likely that this is the clock to which Earnshaw refers. There is no doubt that it is the only regulator known to survive with a dial which provides readings for both temperature and barometric pressure.

The case is of exceptional quality with reeded pilasters on the hood and trunk corners and an extra door on the plinth, which allows access to the pendulum for rating. The composite dial has a middle section of gilt-brass with floral ornament surrounding two white enamel dials, the upper showing seconds, the lower for hours and minutes. To the left is a silvered plate carrying a thermometer calibrated in degrees Fahrenheit and to the right is a mercury barometer with a Vernier scale calibrated in inches.

The weight-driven movement of two-week duration is also of fine quality, with Earnshaw's version of Thomas Mudge's gravity escapement controlled by a nine-bar Harrison gridiron compensation pendulum. This pendulum is unfortunately not the original but a modern replacement of an earlier wood-rod pendulum, which itself would have replaced one of gridiron form. This clock was without doubt one of the more important regulators made at the time and today it has the earliest example of Mudge's detached gravity escapement known to survive.

Purchased in 1989
(Reg. 1989,3–7.1)

William Nicholson

Table regulator
London, 1797
Height 57 cm, width 30.75 cm, depth 17.3 cm

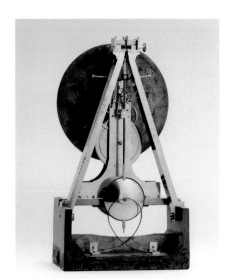

The first gravity escapement was invented by Alexander Cumming (1732–1814) in 1774. This revolutionary escapement for precision regulators is based on the principle of using weighted arms which always fall through the same distance to impulse the pendulum. Consequently, every impulse given is equal in magnitude, giving a more constant rate of oscillation. Cumming's escapement was followed very shortly by Thomas Mudge's, and then a number of other important makers, amongst them William Harvey, introduced their own versions. The advantage of these escapements is that the impulse to the pendulum is constant and not affected by the variations in power from the driving force.

Little is known of William Nicholson who was born in 1753 and lived and worked in London until his death in 1815. This clock, signed on the dial *Wm Nicholson f. 1797*, is a unique piece with Nicholson's own form of gravity escapement invented in 1784. Interestingly, however, he may have involved the clock and watchmaker William Hardy in its production because Hardy's name and address are scratched on the back of the dial *Harday Copice Row* (Hardy's address was 28 Coppice Row, Clerkenwell). The spring-driven movement has Harrison's form of maintaining power to keep the clock going during winding. The clock is unusual in appearance in that the movement is mounted on a massive steel block to provide stability and the pendulum is not suspended from the back of the movement. Instead, two substantial gilded supports rise up from the base and meet at the top to provide a suspensions point for the pendulum. At the top of the supports is Nicholson's unusual form of temperature compensation: a bimetallic block which, as temperature changes, alters its shape to raise or lower the top suspension block and in so doing changes the effective length of the pendulum suspension spring. Another unusual feature is the coiled wire spring which is placed around the pendulum bob to secure it when the clock is being moved.

The elegant satinwood-veneered case has glazed panels at the top, sides and front which reveal the movement from all sides. The case stands on four turned feet and is surmounted by a large urn and flame finial with acanthus decoration. The clock is an interesting example of a rather unassuming case which in reality conceals a movement of a most unusual and interesting design.

Ilbert Collection
(Reg. CAI–1925)

Thomas Mudge

Marine Timekeeper No. 1
London, 1771–4
Height, 7.65 cm, width 13.25 cm, depth 13.25

Thomas Mudge's contribution to the story of marine chronometry took the form of a series of chronometers of which this is the first and is now commonly known as his 'Timekeeper No. 1'. In this amazing machine Mudge introduced a number of new ideas, including the concept of a single mainspring barrel that actually contains two mainsprings operating together in an attempt to provide a more even torque to drive the gear train. More importantly, however, Mudge introduced his 'constant-force' escapement in this marine timekeeper. He had already used a remontoire in his lever clock but here he develops the concept a stage further so that the balance is given a constant impulse at every beat of the escapement.

The dial of this elegant chronometer consists of a gilded-brass dial plate with three white enamel subsidiary dials for hours, minutes and seconds, separated by three pierced and engraved silver scrolled spandrels. At the top is a sector numbered 1–7 flanked by the letters U and D for up and down, to show the state of winding. It was essential at sea that these timekeepers should be wound without fail and should never be allowed to stop through neglect. This example runs for eight days but would have been wound every week.

Equally stylish are its beautifully-made mahogany boxes of octagonal form, the inner with a glazed panel in each facet to reveal the movement, the outer with solid panels and an opening hinged section for access.

In a letter to his patron, Count Maurice von Brühl, dated 23 August 1774, Mudge wrote, 'I acknowledge it [the case] would have been better of brass. My only reason for making it of wood, was to save money, of which I have had, at no time, much to spare'. The machine was tested in private trials at Greenwich between June 1774 and February 1778 but failed because the mainsprings kept breaking. On 1 March 1777 Nevil Maskelyne, the Astronomer Royal, stated that it had gained 1 minute and 19 seconds while on trial at Greenwich for 109 days – an average of less than one second per day. He said that the machine was 'greatly Superior in point of accuracy to any timekeeper which hath come under my inspection'. As a result of its performance Mudge was awarded a payment of £500 by the Board of Longitude. Following a report by a House of Commons Select Committee in 1793, Mudge was awarded a further £3,000, but his death the following year precluded any further work. It was not to be the end of the story, though: using the money, Thomas Mudge junior set up a small manufactory where some twenty-seven copies of his father's chronometer were made.

Ilbert Collection
(Reg. CAI–2119)

John Arnold & Son

Marine chronometer
London, c.1778
Height 10 cm, width 16 cm, depth 16 cm

Arnold watch-paper

John Arnold (CAI–2700)

John Arnold was born in Bodmin, Cornwall, in 1736 and learned the art of watchmaking from his father. He established a business in Devereux Court near Fleet Street, London, and very soon became a highly respected member of the horological community. This was partly achieved by the making of an extraordinary quarter-repeating watch for George III in 1764. Made in the form of a finger ring, it measured no more than one-third of an inch in diameter (c.8.5 mm) and yet consisted of more than 120 components. One of the most demanding pieces in this incredible watch was the ruby cylinder for the escapement. A hollow tube of ruby with part of the walls cut away, it measured just one fifty-fourth of an inch in diameter (less than 0.5 mm).

Arnold's business thrived and became one of the favourites of wealthy clients from England and abroad, enabling Arnold to devote his skills to the matter of marine timekeeping. In 1771 he began working on a pivoted-detent escapement and the following year his third chronometer was taken on board the *Resolution* to serve Captain James Cook on his second voyage of discovery. In comparison with Harrison's extraordinary chronometer H4, Arnold's machines were simple but equally effective. In 1782 Arnold was granted a patent for a new spring-detent escapement, and the following year Thomas Earnshaw's spring-detent escapement was patented in the name of Thomas Wright, his sponsor, an event which began a long and bitter dispute between the two giants in the field of marine timekeeping at the end of the eighteenth century.

Arnold's achievement can be seen in the form of new and accurate marine chronometers using an escapement which needed no oil, and balances which had temperature compensation built into their design. This chronometer is typical and was made in 1790, by which time Arnold's son John Roger was working with him. It has a fusee, a going train of four wheels and an Arnold spring-detent escapement with a temperature compensation balance of Arnold's design, known from its shape as the 'YZ' type. In this, the free arms of the rim are made from bimetallic strips with platinum on the outside and a copper, zinc and silver alloy on the inside, so that changes in temperature will cause the arms to move in or out to compensate for changes in elasticity in the balance spring.

The movement is signed on the back plate *John Arnold & Son, London Nº 14/104*, indicating that this chronometer, number 14, was later improved by Arnold and at that time re-numbered 104. This chronometer served an important role. In April 1791 George Vancouver (1757–1798) set sail with two ships, the *Discovery* and the *Chatham*, to continue the work of James Cook in his search for the north-west passage. Between 1791 and 1795, along with four other timekeepers, Arnold's No.14 played an essential part in establishing longitude and carrying out detailed surveying of the Pacific coastline of North America.

Ilbert Collection
(Reg. CAI–2069)

Thomas Earnshaw

Marine chronometer no. 509
London, c.1800
Height 17.6 cm, width 20.8 cm, depth 20.8 cm

Thomas Earnshaw

John Arnold's rival in the protracted argument over who first invented the spring-detent escapement was Thomas Earnshaw. Born in Ashton-under-Lyne in 1749, Earnshaw served an apprenticeship in London which he completed in 1770; he then worked as a trade watch-finisher and escapement maker of extraordinary ability. In contrast to John Arnold, who had a somewhat privileged early career, Earnshaw came up the hard way. He married before he had finished his apprenticeship and within four years had three sons. By 1774 he was facing the debtors' prison and fled to Ireland, but in the end his conscience overcame him and he returned to the Fleet Prison in December 1774. By 1780 he had seemingly cleared his debts and was running a successful business which allowed him to concern himself with improvements to the pivoted detent escapement. From this work came his version of the spring-detent escapement. In May 1782, however, Arnold was granted a patent that included his version of the spring-detent escapement and it was not until February 1783 that Earnshaw's escapement received a patent in the name of Thomas Wright, who registered the design on Earnshaw's behalf.

An Earnshaw chronometer is simplicity itself with a movement comprised of a spring-barrel and fusee driving a four-wheel gear train and an escapement consisting of escape wheel, spring-detent, gold passing spring and jewelled impulse and discharge rollers. The operation of the escapement is controlled by a temperature-compensated balance with split rims on which are screwed two moveable weights which provide temperature compensation. The balance also has a helical blued-steel balance spring. The dial indicates hours, minutes and seconds and the whole machine is housed in a simple wooden box with gimbal mounts to keep it level irrespective of the motion of the ship.

This one-day chronometer, made in about 1800, is signed *Thos Earnshaw Inv^t et Fecit N° 509 London N° 2853*. During its illustrious history it served on a number of Royal Navy ships until June 1830 when it returned on HMS *Hector* with Captain J. Bolder after a period of seven years in service. In July 1830 it went to Robert Molyneux for cleaning and overhaul and was back at Greenwich ready for use again in November that same year. It was not issued to any ship until March 1831 when it was delivered to Devonport, where its rate was checked. In December of that year it went into service, along with a number of other chronometers, on HMS *Beagle*'s momentous voyage with Captain Robert Fitzroy and Charles Darwin.

Ilbert Collection
(Reg. CAI–1957)

Breguet et Fils

Marine chronometer
Paris, 1813
Height 12.55 cm, width 17.4 cm, depth 17.4 cm

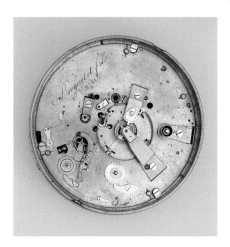

Towards the end of the eighteenth century, improvements in the time-keepers used for finding longitude at sea were, to a large extent, achieved by English chronometer makers, particularly John Arnold and Thomas Earnshaw. Nevertheless, the great French clockmakers were also striving for the same goal and makers such as Ferdinand Berthoud, Pierre Leroy and Henri Motel all played their part. The most celebrated French watch-maker, Abraham Louis Breguet, was involved in the quest and made a number of marine chronometers.

This example was never used at sea. When completed in 1813 Breguet used it himself as an experimental workshop piece until 1822. The chronometer has a lever escapement and also an independent timer for minutes and seconds. The silver dial shows the hours and minutes on the left and has a chapter ring with seconds in the top centre, but there are also dials on the right for independent minute- and seconds-timing and two sectors at the bottom which show the state of wind of the two mainsprings.

The box is made from mahogany with gimbal mounts for the drum which holds the chronometer. Unusually, there are two spring-loaded wood screws attached to the box, which are provided to allow the chronometer to be fixed to a flat wooden surface. When not used they are retracted within the perimeter of the box and held there by springs. A key is provided which has two squares for releasing the gimbal lock and also for turning the wood screws. A second ratchet or 'tipsy' key is used to wind the chronometer. It runs for more than thirty-five hours but would have been wound every day.

After being used as a test-bed to try the performance of different components it was finally presented to Breguet's friend Monseigneur Louis Belmas (1757–1841), Bishop of Cambrai, to whom it is inscribed, *Premiere Piece ou la Comunication du Rouage au Régulateur S'Opère Sans Frotement. Exécutée en 1813 par Breguet Pour Mr Belmas ami de l'auteur No2741* ('The first piece in which the transmission from the train to the regulator occurs without friction. Made in 1813 by Breguet for Mr. Belmas friend of the author'). Emmanuel Breguet, in *Breguet, Watch-makers Since 1775*, paints a wonderful picture of Belmas as a collector who spent nearly 20,000 francs on Breguet watches between 1814 and 1822 and who described them in his letters to Breguet in the most affectionate terms.

Breguet's aim in this piece was to incorporate an escapement in which there was no sliding friction produced at the point of impulse to the balance. This he achieved with limited success for, while it is true in one respect, he nevertheless introduced other frictions into the impulse geometry, which negated what he had accomplished.

Ilbert Collection
(Reg. CAI–2066)

134

Breguet et Fils

Astronomer's follower clock
Paris, c.1815
Height 42.5 cm, width 18.5 cm, depth 16.8 cm

Abraham Louis Breguet, born in 1747 in Neuchâtel in Switzerland, was without doubt one of the most ingenious of watch- and clockmakers. At the age of eighteen he moved to Paris, then to Versailles where he studied with the watchmaker Etienne Gide. In 1775 he married Cécile L'Huillier and established his own business at Quai de l'Horloge in Paris in partnership with Xavier Gide, the brother of his former master. He very quickly rose to eminence, becoming Clockmaker to Louis XVI, and was soon supplying watches and clocks to the nobility of Europe. He suffered problems during the French Revolution and spent time in exile in Switzerland but when France settled down during the Empire under Napoleon Bonaparte he returned and became Clockmaker to the Emperor. He took his son Louis-Antoine into partnership in 1820 and, following his death in 1823, Louis continued the business, which produced some of the finest watches made in the nineteenth century and still exists today.

For their observations, astronomers needed a precision regulator. In some instances, however, they might also make use of a timekeeper which struck a bell at second intervals which could be used to time observations when the astronomer was working alone. Of the few examples of these clocks which do survive, this is perhaps the most sophisticated. It contains refinements rarely found in precision table regulators and is one of just two clocks made by Breguet which survive today. This clock has a constant-force escapement of Breguet's own design with the impulse provided by a falling platinum weight. A gridiron pendulum provides compensation for changes in temperature.

The rear case panel is numbered 04813 and the number '4' appears on some of the components suggesting that a batch of clocks were made. Indeed, George Daniels in *The Art of Breguet* illustrates a clock numbered '3', bought by Breguet from a Monsieur Lolloé and then improved by Monsieur de Proney, who added the latitude compensator.

The woods chosen for the plain mahogany case are finely figured, giving the clock a simple but elegant appearance with only a moulding around the top and an extended plinth to add weight to the overall effect. The dial is simple with an outer enamel ring for the centre-seconds hand and a subsidiary enamel dial in the lower part for hours and minutes. In the upper centre a glazed aperture reveals Breguet's escapement.

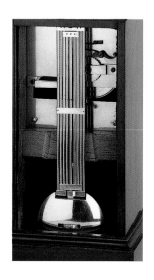

The unusual and sophisticated feature of the clock, however, is the glass dome at the top, which reveals two small balls at the end of a bar mounted horizontally at the very top of the pendulum rod. The position of these balls affects the rate of the pendulum by only tiny amounts, but moving them in or out from the centre is enough to compensate for the variations in the force of gravity, which is strongest at the poles and weakest at the equator. A scale inside the dome, calibrated 0–90, allows the bar-and-ball compensator to be adjusted according to the latitude where the clock is being used.

Ilbert Collection
(Reg. CAI–2122)

Abraham Louis Breguet

Humpback carriage clock with alarm
Paris, *c.*1820
Height 15.5 cm, width 12.1 cm, depth 6 cm

Abraham Louis Breguet is said to have been the inventor of the carriage clock, which usually took the form of a clock in a metal framed case glazed on all four sides, with a carrying handle at the top. For his highest quality carriage clocks, however, Breguet used a case of individual design consisting of a round-topped 'humpback' case with silver chains at the top for carrying. The firm of Breguet et Fils made these carriage clocks between about 1812 and 1830 and this particular example of 1822 is typical. It was sold to a Colonel Cook on 7 October 1822 for 4,800 francs, at the time a tidy sum of money.

This superbly-made, spring-driven clock has a duration of eight days and a detached lever escapement. It is of a typically elegant Breguet design with a fine engine-turned dial-plate which provides a restrained background for the various dials and subsidiaries. It indicates hours and minutes on the main dial, and has a subsidiary seconds dial below XII as well as further subsidiaries for the age and phase of the moon on the left and for alarm setting on the right. In addition to striking the hours in passing, there is also a repeat mechanism which strikes the half-quarters and the hours on steel-wire gongs when a chain is pulled. In order to save space, the wire gongs are carefully curved to follow the shape of the movement. Below the main dial is a perpetual calendar with four apertures showing the days of the week, the date, the month and the year. The sophisticated calendar mechanism automatically adjusts for the leap years.

The clock is signed on the movement *Breguet et Fils H^grs de la Marine Royale No. 3629*. However, this is curiously engraved on a separate piece of brass, which is fairly crudely soldered into the back plate. It is difficult to accept that this could have been done in Breuget's workshops. On the other hand, all the French case marks are correct for this carriage clock, which is clearly not an accidental marriage of movement, dial and case.

The silver case has the maker's mark LA L with a fleur-de-lys above and a star below, probably the mark of the Parisian silversmith Louis Legay whose business was near Breguet's in Quai de L'Horloge. This characteristic Breguet design of clock was copied in London and a number of examples survive made by the partnership of James Ferguson Cole and his brother Thomas and also by Joseph Jump (1827–1899).

S.E. Prestige Collection
Purchased in 1969
(Reg. 1969,3–3.3)

Bust of Abraham Louis Breguet
Ilbert Collection
(Reg. CAI-3396)

Edward Funnell

Table regulator
Brighton, *c.*1860
Height 48.5 cm, width 31.5 cm, depth 14 cm

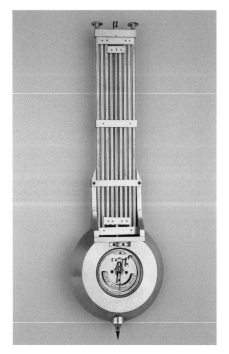

In *Clockmakers of Sussex*, E.J. Tyler tells us that Edward Funnell was born in Brighton and baptised there in April 1822. He was married in 1843 but remarried in 1850. He is described as very short in stature. In 1850 he had a business at 2 Clarence Place, Brighton, but between 1862 and 1878 could be found at 54 East Street. He is known to have exhibited what was described as 'The smallest Watch in the world' which was only seven-sixteenths of an inch in diameter (11.112 mm) and an eighth of an inch thick (3.175 mm), with ten jewelled bearing holes and five other ruby actions. He exhibited the same watch, together with carriage clocks, at the 1855 Paris Exhibition, where he was awarded an 'honourable mention' for it. In complete contrast, he is also known to have installed turret clocks in a number of public buildings and churches, including Newick and Chailey (both in East Sussex) and Winkleigh in Devon. He died in 1889.

A measure of Funnell's ability can be seen in this unique mantel regulator which incorporates a sophisticated remontoire spring-detent escapement. In essence the escapement is similar to a normal spring-detent escapement, but here the escape wheel is mounted on a frame together with the spring-detent. Instead of being unlocked by an oscillating balance, the unlocking is performed by the pendulum. After unlocking, a series of wheels on the front plate are allowed to rotate, and in so doing provide a constant force to the escape wheel, which imparts an impulse to the pendulum to keep it swinging. As the pendulum continues its swing it resets the escape wheel carriage so that the escape wheel locks again on the locking stone of the detent. On its return swing, the pendulum simply flips the passing spring as the balance does in a normal spring-detent escapement. The sophisticated gridiron pendulum compensates for temperature changes and also has a thermometer mounted in the bob.

There is no case as such but the clock was originally protected by a glass dome, allowing all of the mechanism to be seen. The clock of skeleton form, with heavily-gilded plates, is mounted on a black marble base with a gilded plinth and scrolled feet. The double dial consists of an upper chapter ring with centre-seconds hand, which encloses the visible escapement and a lower dial for hours and minutes. The centre of this dial is decorated with an intricate foliate design enclosing a cartouche which was originally inscribed:

Remontoire Chronometer
Designed and Made By
Edward Funnell
BRIGHTON

Ilbert Collection
(Reg. CAI–2133)

Anonymous

Early Japanese stand/lantern clock
Japan, seventeenth/eighteenth century
Base: height 97 cm, width 55.5 cm, depth 55.5 cm
Clock: height 43.5 cm, width 16.5 cm, depth 16.5 cm

In 1549 Francis Xavier, a Portuguese Jesuit missionary, arrived at Kagoshima and the following year applied to the local governor for permission to establish a Jesuit mission there. To help negotiations, he presented the governor with a clock. This was followed by further gifts of clocks by other missionaries, the most famous of which was a clock made in Madrid in 1581. By the early seventeenth century, however, the activities of the missionaries were considered detrimental to Japanese culture and all were expelled, leaving the country effectively closed to western influences for more than two centuries. In the seventeenth century the Japanese began making their own clocks, at first in imitation of sixteenth-century European chamber clocks, but soon a style developed which was exclusively Japanese. Such clocks remained fashionable until the end of the rule of the Tokugawa Shogun in 1866. In 1873, following the opening up of trade with western Europe, the system of twenty-four equal hours beginning at midnight was adopted.

Until 1873, time in Japan was measured in unequal hours with the day divided into periods of daylight and darkness, and each of these periods divided into six equal parts called *toki*. Thus, in winter, the daylight 'hours' would be short and the darkness 'hours' long and vice versa in summer. The day began at dusk and on just two days of the year, at the vernal and autumnal equinoxes, the day and night 'hours' would be the same and equal to two European hours. At all other times the length of the hours would gradually change through the year. Each *toki* was also assigned a zodiac in the sequence, horse 9 (midday) followed by sheep 8, monkey 7, cock 6 (sunset), dog 5, wild boar 4, rat 9 (midnight), ox 8, tiger 7, hare 6 (sunrise), dragon 5 and snake 4.

This clock, made in about 1700, has an oscillating foliot with adjustable weights. Called *Yagura-Dokei*, meaning tower clocks, they still used the standard 1–12 blows on the bell to indicate the passing hours which would have meant nothing in Japan at the time where the hours were numbered 9, 8, 7, 6, 5, 4, twice. Clearly, in order for these clocks to indicate unequal hours in any way correctly, the rate of the clock would have to be adjusted by moving the weights on the foliot, not only according to the time of year but also at sunrise and sunset on a daily basis. Such constant alteration was clearly not practical and it is likely that in feudal Japan in the seventeenth century clocks were simply owned as expensive curiosities rather than as instruments for measuring time. An interesting feature is the four chrysanthemum flowers on the front which suggest that the clock was originally an imperial piece.

The clock stands on a rare black lacquered pyramidal base inlaid with mother-of-pearl decoration incorporating a Chinese poem. 'In place of an expected pot, this present instrument will give the hour & division, correctly presenting heaven's word.' It is known that this base, although contemporary with the clock, was married to it by J. Drummond Robertson in the 1930s.

Drummond Robertson Collection
Ilbert Collection
(Reg. CAI–2165)

Anonymous

Pillar/musical bracket clocks
Japan, eighteenth/nineteenth centuries
Table clock: height 17 cm, width 15.8 cm, depth 9.8 cm
Pillar clock: height 51.5 cm, width 8.2 cm, depth 7 cm

Two major problems existed in the early form of Japanese lantern clocks: firstly, that they struck the wrong hours and secondly that they needed constant adjustment in order to show unequal hours. To solve the first problem was a simple matter of devising a suitable count-wheel which would produce a striking sequence of 9, 8, 7, 6, 5, 4, 9, 8, 7, 6, 5, 4, and by the mid-eighteenth century such clocks were commonplace.

A more difficult problem was that of indicating the unequal hours and here the Japanese were ingenious in devising two different methods to achieve it. In the first system, the solution was to make the dial rotate and have a series of 'hour' and 'half-hour' plates which were adjustable. A fixed central hand indicated the time, and at regular intervals the arrangement of the indicators on the dial would have to be adjusted to show the relative lengths of the day and night hours. In some clocks, the day hour plaques were silver and the night hour plaques were of darkened metal.

Another way of solving the problem was to have two foliots, one at the top for the daylight 'hours' and the lower one for the night 'hours'. In these clocks it is the progress of the striking train which changes the control from one foliot to the other. This system was commonly used on later lantern clocks and table clocks (*makura-dokei*) such as the one illustrated here which has a fixed chapter ring with a rotating central disc and hand. The series of holes around the central disc are for a pin to be inserted to release the alarm at the desired time.

Another form of Japanese clock which appeared in the nineteenth century was the pillar clock (*shaku-dokei*) which was designed to fit on the narrow interior pillars of a Japanese house. Here the method of indicating the hours could be one or both of two ways. In the first method, as in this weight-driven clock, the hour numerals are moveable to indicate the unequal hours, but an ingenious method has been devised to enable the clock to strike at the appropriate time. The time indicators, arranged vertically down the dial, have long studs at the back and the driving weight, which descends inside the case, is the striking mechanism. As it passes behind a particular hour indicator, it will be released by the projecting stud to strike the appropriate hour. Clocks of this type may also have a series of seven lacquered plates with scales to show the hours, six double-sided and one single-sided plate, for different times of the year. These would need to be changed every two weeks to suit the time of year. The plate on this clock shows a winter period with the 'hours' between sunset and sunrise close together.

Drummond Robertson Collection/
Ilbert Collection
(Table clock Reg. CAI–2022)
(Pillar clock Reg. 1975 12-2 1)

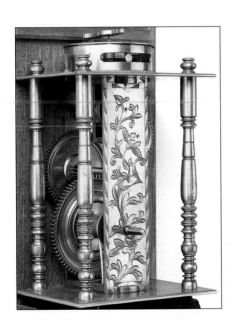

Dwerrihouse & Co

Tavern clock
London, *c.*1810
Dial diameter 55 cm, overall height 116.5 cm, depth 17.5 cm

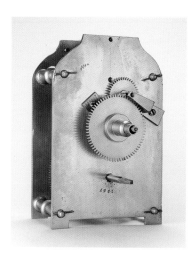

Trade card of John Dwerrihouse

On 19 July 1797 William Pitt's government passed an Act of Parliament which levied a tax on clocks and watches:

> Anno Tricessimo Septimo
> Georgii III Regis
> Cap. CVIII
> An Act for granting to His Majesty certain Duties on
> Clocks and Watches   [19 July 1797]

> For and upon every Clock or Timekeeper, by whatever Name the same shall be called, which shall be used for the Purpose of a Clock, and placed in or upon any Dwelling House, or any Office or Building thereunto belonging, or any other Building whatever, whether private or publick, belonging to any Person or Persons, or Company of Persons, or any Body Corporate or Politick, or Collegiate, or which shall be kept and used, by any Person or Persons in Great Britain, there shall be charged an Annual Duty of Five Shillings

Further charges were made on watches depending on their quality: ten shillings for gold watches and five shillings for silver- or base-metal-cased watches. It seems that in response to the Act everyone hid their clocks and watches to avoid payment and it was repealed the following year as impractical.

The Act would have been largely forgotten except for the fact that it led to a misnomer for a group of clocks, which for many years were referred to as 'Act of Parliament clocks'. The fact that the existence of these large-dialled timepiece wall clocks can be traced back to many years earlier than the Act has resulted in them now being referred to more correctly as 'tavern clocks'. Traditionally, the tavern clock was a large-dialled clock, designed for use in taverns and other public buildings. They were often housed in lacquered cases with chinoiserie decoration on the front.

This particular example is one which comes from the end of the story of the true tavern clock. Here the case is made from fine mahogany with a very large dial (55 cm across) and with large spade-pattern brass hands. It is a wall-mounted eight-day timepiece with anchor escapement and pendulum, driven by a large cast-iron weight of wedge-shape, to allow it to descend as far down the case as possible.

The clock is signed on the dial *Dwerrihouse Berkeley Square*, a firm of clock- and watchmakers whose business was in Mayfair, London, and was founded by John Dwerrihouse in about 1770. The company continued after John Dwerrihouse's death in 1805, with partnerships between his successors and Carter between 1800 and 1827, Bell between 1825 and 1875, and also Ogston & Bell. The movement is numbered 5261. The company is known to have used Thwaites of Clerkenwell as suppliers and it is very likely that this clock was made by them for Dwerrihouse. They are known to have supplied John Dwerrihouse with thirty-three clocks, and No. 5261 can be dated to 1814.

Purchased in 1982
(Reg. 1982,5–11.1)

Santiago James Moore French

Rolling Ball Clock
Royal Exchange, London, *c.*1830
Height 61 cm, base width 43 cm, depth 43 cm

ABOVE CENTRE: watch-paper of Santiago James Moore French

Sir William Congreve (1772–1828) was the second son of Lieutenant General Sir William Congreve. Like his father, he was a military man serving in the Royal Artillery. As Comptroller of the Woolwich Laboratory he developed rockets first used in naval attacks on the French fleet at Boulogne Harbour in 1805 and 1806. In later life he was Member of Parliament for Plymouth (1820–1828) but is perhaps best known for some ingenious inventions, including a colour printing system. In the horological world his name lives on in the form of a clock controlled by a steel ball rolling down a sloped track. He was granted a patent in 1808 for his 'extreme detached escapement' and his rolling ball clock. The original weight-driven clock can still be seen in the Rotunda building of the Royal Artillery Museum at the Woolwich Arsenal.

Although his clock was a serious attempt to improve timekeeping, it was anything but successful in that respect. On the other hand, the design found immediate popularity, and clocks incorporating it have been made by numerous makers from the early nineteenth century to this day. While many see these clocks as an attempt at perpetual motion, there is no mystery involved. The ball rolling down the track does not drive the clock, but simply determines the rate at which the clock runs. Each time the ball reaches the end of its run it hits a release lever which unlocks the grooved tray. The power of the mainspring is then transmitted through a train of gears which tilts the tray and locks it so that the ball then begins its journey back down the track until it reaches the bottom and triggers the release to repeat the process. The ball is timed to take just thirty seconds to make its journey, but all manner of influences such as temperature change, humidity change and dust on the track conspire to make these clocks bad timekeepers.

This particular clock, in a most elegant satinwood case, is glazed all round and with a large glass dome at the top. It was made in about 1830 by the firm of Santiago James Moore French, whose business was at 15 Sweetings Alley, Royal Exchange, London, and it is signed *French Royal Exchange London 470*. The three dials indicate hours on the left, minutes in the middle and seconds on the right, although the seconds hand moves from 60 to 30 and so on as the table tilts and does not show actual seconds. A more detailed seconds indicator exists in the form of a slide above the table where the seconds are indicated through a series of small windows, 0, 5, 10, 15, 20, 25, 30 and, when the table tilts, the slide moves to show 30–60 in five-second intervals.

Ilbert Collection
(Reg. CAI–2137)

RIGHT: Sir William Congreve

Adey B. Savory & Sons

Skeleton clock
London, c.1860
Height 33 cm, width 25.5 cm, depth 15 cm

Premises of 14 Cornhill

The skeleton clock is characterized by having its movement plates pierced out to a minimum of essential metal in a symmetrical design which leaves all the wheel-work and escapement clearly visible. Rather than having a case, the clock is then housed under a glass dome so that the intricacies of the machine are exposed for all to see. In nineteenth-century England these clocks became a familiar sight on the tables and mantelpieces of middle- and upper-class homes. Although there is great debate about their origins and discussion concerning the fact that many of them are unsigned, their popularity is in no doubt. The first skeleton clocks were made in France towards the end of the eighteenth century but there were also a small number of unusual clocks made in England, such as Joseph Merlin's unique 1776 clock, which is now displayed at Kenwood House on Hampstead Heath in London, and Sir William Congreve's 'extreme detached escapement' clock of 1808 in the Royal Collections.

However, the skeleton clock in the form in which it became commonly known in England appeared in the 1820s, following a French fashion. These clocks appear to have been produced by a relatively small number of businesses based particularly in London, Liverpool and Birmingham. Large-scale manufacturers such as John Smith & Sons of Clerkenwell and James Condliff of Liverpool supplied a multitude of retailers who added their names to the dials. The clocks' individual styles ranged from the simple timepiece, perhaps with the added sophistication of a one-at-the-hour strike on a bell at the top, to grandiose chiming clocks with plates pierced out in the form of English cathedrals, particularly York Minster and Lichfield Cathedral. The clocks were commonly designed to go for eight days but year-going examples were also made. The popularity of the design continued throughout the Victorian era but declined in the twentieth century, although even today booklets can be purchased giving complete instructions on how to make one, using simple machinery and hand tools.

This small skeleton clock is of simple design with a timepiece movement with anchor escapement. The plates are cast in a symmetrical design to accommodate the mainspring barrel, fusee, gear train and escapement. The pendulum is suspended in the normal way at the back of the clock, and the chapter ring is signed *A.B. Savory & Co. Cornhill.* This large company was described in directories as being watch and clockmakers, goldsmiths, dealers in foreign coin and bullion.

Presented by Jeremy Evans in 1998
(Reg. 1998, 12-2.1)

Johann Baptist Beha

Cuckoo clock
Eisenbach, Germany, c.1870
Height 45.1 cm, width 25 cm, depth 15 cm

A question often asked of the horological curator is 'when was the first cuckoo clock made?' The first answer which comes to many people's minds is a result of a comment made by the character Harry Lime in the 1949 film *The Third Man*, where he says 'In Italy for thirty years under the Borgias they had warfare, terror, murder and bloodshed but they produced Michelangelo, Leonardo da Vinci and the Renaissance. In Switzerland, they had brotherly love; they had five hundred years of democracy and peace and what did that produce? The cuckoo clock.' Nothing could be further from the truth, although the origins of this most famous of wall-clocks still remain a mystery. Possible makers of the earliest examples are Franz Anton Ketterer of Schönwald and Josef Kammerer of Furtwangen. It has also been suggested that these clocks have their origins further east, in Bohemia. Indeed, the Horst Landrock Collection in Germany contains one of the oldest cuckoo clocks, dated to c.1750, which has a marked similarity to clocks made in Bohemia at the time. While the precise origins of this type of clock remain obscure, there can be no doubt that it was in the Black Forest (Schwarzwald) area of south Germany where their production became popular, and from where they were exported in huge numbers around the world.

This weight-driven, wooden-framed cuckoo clock, made by Johann Baptist Beha (1815–1898), runs for thirty hours. Beha's clockmaking business was based in Eisenbach in the Black Forest. It has a case in a neo-Gothic architectural style which unusually retains almost all its original features, including the carved pendulum, cuckoo door and cresting to the roof gable. Although it is of simple construction, the design and methods behind its assembly are remarkably good. A feature peculiar to Beha clocks is that the bottom, front and top beech-wood plates are all secured using a heavy threaded bolt, presumably to resist any movement in the wooden plates. The basic structure of the case is interesting as the cuckoo and bellows lids are not enclosed under a roof, as became the practice in later clocks. It also has a semicircular backboard, similar to those found on the older style *Schild* dial cuckoo clocks, but above the dial it has the gable roof of the later *Bahnhausle* style. In later clocks this roof was extended at the back to cover the whole movement.

Purchased in 1995
(Reg. 1995,1–12.2)

Jerome & Company

Shelf-clock
New Haven, Connecticut, c.1880
Height 65 cm, width 39 cm, depth 10.5 cm

In 1802, Eli Terry erected a workshop near Plymouth, Connecticut, and proceeded to manufacture wooden clock movements with machine-made components. Using his new system of batch production he could make clocks far more quickly and more cheaply than any of his rival clock-makers in New England. He went on to develop and enlarge the process to such an extent that he was soon making over two-hundred clocks per year. Terry's production of longcase clock movements expanded even further when he designed and built a much bigger factory to supply four-hundred movements for an order from Edward and Levi Porter. In his second year of operation he produced more than a thousand pieces. After further expansion, Terry moved to the production of shelf clocks, which soon ended the popularity of the longcase clock in America.

Following Terry's pioneering work, by the middle of the nineteenth century American clocks were being made in huge numbers. It was then only a matter of time before these cheap and simple clocks would be exported. Of the many entrepreneurs who became involved in the industry, Chauncey Jerome was one of the most influential. He was by trade a case-maker and responsible for ideas and designs which influenced the trade for many years, but he also hit upon the idea of producing thirty-hour brass clocks very cheaply.

Jerome's first attempts to establish an export market in England, however, were not initially successful. With his son Chauncey Epaphroditus Peck, he sent his first consignment of clocks to England in the summer of 1842. The clocks were seized by customs officers who, suspicious of their incredibly low value, compulsorily purchased them. A second shipment was similarly treated but the third was allowed to enter the country, and so began a flood of American clocks which was to compete with the Black Forest industry and damage still further what remained of the British clockmaking industry.

This is one such clock made by Jerome & Company. It has a brass, thirty-hour movement mounted in an ogee-form case. The driving weights are housed inside the case, making it suitable for a mantelpiece. These new designs also had colourful reverse painted glass panels in the lower half of the glazed door. Opening the case reveals a pasted-on label with a picture of the factory where the clock was made and detailed instructions for setting the clock up and adjusting its rate. With clocks as cheap as this, often supplied through mail order catalogues, there was no question of after-sales service.

Presented by Mrs Nora Evans in 1998
(Reg. 1998,12–3.1)

RIGHT: Chauncey Jerome

André Romain Guilmet

Mystery clock
Paris, *c*.1880
Height 61 cm, width 27 cm, depth 20 cm

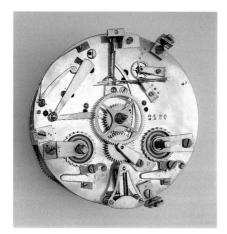

In the horological world, the name A.R. Guilmet is associated with the so-called 'mystery' clocks, which to this day fascinate the uninitiated as to how they work. Guilmet was granted a French patent for his invention in 1867, which was modified in 1872. The 1867 patent or 'Brevet' was to run for fifteen years for a 'Pendule à marche mystérieuse'. That the clocks were popular is perhaps reflected in the fact that they were displayed at major international exhibitions such as the one held in Paris in 1878. Guilmet is one of a number of French mystery-clock makers. The most important and successful of them was Jean Eugène Robert-Houdin (1805–1871), a conjurer who also made mystery clocks, the best-known of which were his glass-dialled clocks with a magical hand that had no visible means of propulsion; Harry Houdini, the great American escapologist, named himself after Houdin.

A.R. Guilmet was a man of many talents, involved in a variety of mechanical and scientific pursuits, including electric motors and bicycle chains. In horology, his best-known contribution is the form of mystery clock seen here. The pendulum swings back and forth with no obvious impulse to keep it going, as its only connection with the clock and the driving mechanism is the spring which suspends the pendulum from the outstretched hand of the figure.

What happens in practice is that the figure stands on a circular, pivoted platform which moves imperceptibly by about 0.5 mm from side to side, a movement which is enough to keep the pendulum swinging. While the impulse for the pendulum is coming through the suspension spring, the length of the pendulum still affects the rate at which it swings and it still determines the rate at which the escapement operates. In a clock where the mystery lies in the fact that there is no apparent connection between the clock and pendulum, it seems strange to have an original glass dial which reveals the operation of the mechanism. The escapement which keeps the figure swinging is also a Guilmet invention devised specifically for these clocks. It consists of a pallet assembly which is caused to move back and forth by the motion of the pendulum. At the same time a cranked revolving arm is turned by the gear train and alternately locks and unlocks on the pallets. Through this device the turning motion, back and forth, is imparted to the standing figure on the top. The clock also strikes the hours on a bell mounted at the back of the movement.

Ilbert Collection
(Reg. CAI–2056)

James Brock

Longcase regulator
London, c.1880
Height 225 cm, width 48.5 cm, depth 30.5 cm

In March 1859, having been tested and refined in the workshops of E.J. Dent, the Great Clock (Big Ben to the uninitiated) at the Palace of Westminster was finally installed and working. The mechanism of this world-famous clock had been designed by Edmund Beckett Denison (Lord Grimthorpe) to specifications laid down by George Biddle Airy (1801–1892), the Astronomer Royal. Work had begun on the clock in 1852 after an eight-year dispute with Benjamin Lewis Vulliamy, who lost the contract for building the clock largely because he would not submit plans and estimates until two years after the tender for the clock was put out by the government.

It was the foreman in Dent's workshops, a man called James Brock, who oversaw the construction of that enormous machine. Brock later left Dent's employ and set up in business on his own account in George Street, Portman Square, London, and it was here that this regulator was made.

In many ways this clock is old-fashioned in its appearance, with a traditional hooded case in a longcase style which to a large extent had died out as a fashion in London. However, the light-coloured wood for the case and the bold egg-and-dart moulding at the top show it to date from about 1880 when it would have made an excellent addition to any fine jeweller's shop.

The movement shows Brock's connection with the Westminster clock in having a four-legged gravity escapement of Grimthorpe's design and a zinc-iron compensated pendulum. The massive plates show that typical disregard for economy of materials in the Victorian era. The weight line passes up above the movement over a barrel/pulley in order to keep the weight to the side clear of the pendulum and escapement arms.

James Brock died in 1893 at the age of sixty-seven. Lord Grimthorpe later referred to him in a letter he wrote to the *Horological Journal* in 1902, concerning his gravity escapement:

> I am sitting now in front of the very first of them, which was made straight off from my drawing in 1852, and it has been going ever since, either in London, while I kept a house there, or here. I am sorry to say that its actual maker, James Brock is dead. He was an excellent and charming man, who first worked for me at the original Dent's, in the Strand, and who built a sufficient factory in a stable-yard in that region, where we made the Westminster clock and sundry other large ones.

Purchased in 1988
(Reg. 1988,5–1.1)

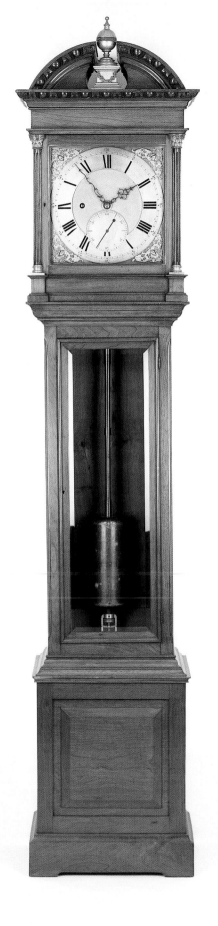

Nicole Nielsen

Carriage clock
London, c.1915
Height 16 cm, width 9.5 cm, depth 6.5 cm

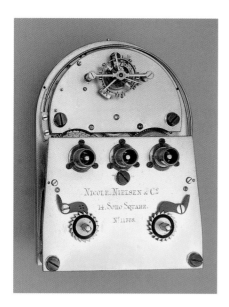

14 Soho Square

By the beginning of the twentieth century the carriage clock already had a long history. In many ways, with some notable exceptions, the general quality of carriage clocks had deteriorated since Abraham Louis Breguet's pioneering work. In stark contrast to the off-the-peg variety commonly available is this masterpiece of clockmaking by the renowned firm Nicole Nielsen of 14 Soho Square, London. Adolphe Nicole and Emil Nielsen had a reputation second to none in the field of high-quality clock- and watchmaking. The firm became famous for its use of precision machinery in the production of clocks and watches, which were made not only for their own retail but also for many other leading London makers and retailers.

This particular clock is signed *Nicole Nielsen & Co. 14 Soho Square London no.11558*. It is a small silver-cased, eight-day carriage clock which is to some extent based on the Breguet 'pendule de voyage' design described on page 140. There are the usual dials for hours, minutes and seconds, but in addition there are two 'up-and-down' dials which show the state of winding of the two mainsprings. The movement has a lever escapement with a one-minute revolving tourbillon; the escapement is mounted on a carriage which constantly revolves. This idea, introduced by Abraham Louis Breguet in the late eighteenth century, was intended to remove timekeeping errors caused in the oscillating balance when the clock is put in different positions. By constantly changing the position of the escapement and balance, the errors are averaged out. This small clock also has optional grande-sonnerie or petite-sonnerie striking, the former striking the hours and quarters at every quarter, the latter striking the quarters alone and the hour on the hour. As a final sophistication it can be made to repeat the last hour and quarter at the press of a button. It is protected whilst travelling by a leather carrying-case.

The clock dates from the beginning of the twentieth century, probably about 1905, and is one of a group of ten such clocks, some of which were made for the well-known firm of Frodshams in London. They are numbered from 11553–11559.

Purchased in 1987
(Reg. 1987,11–3.1)

American Electrical and Novelty & Manufacturing Company

Ever-Ready ticket clock
New York, c.1930
Height 16.2 cm, diameter 8.75 cm

In 1902 Eugene Fitsch took out an American patent for a clock in which the time is indicated on a series of 'tickets' which flip over to indicate the time in digital form. The design was also registered in England on 18 September 1902, as follows (spec.no. 20.371):

> *Chronoscopes.* Relates to the exhibition of a succession of indicating or advertising plates and is particularly described as a chronoscopic advertising clock. Such time indications as are shown by Figs. 4, 5 and 6 are presented by two sets of sixty plates *a* hinged to two drums *i*, Fig. 3, one of which rotates once per hour and the other once in twelve hours. The shaft *f* on which the drums turn is slightly inclined rearwards, and the cards, successively escaping from the spring-set stops *p*, swing over to a trap *v* first by resilience and then by gravity; as follows from their number, an hour plate escapes every twelve minutes, and in the hour between the 'half pasts' five of them are haft alike. The shaft *f* is supported in a hollow base by a ball bearing, and the clock movement contained in the base is thus relieved of weight. The shaft protruding into the base is connected with the minute arbor by a clutch. The hour drum, is upon a sleeve, and motion work is provided between the shaft and the sleeve. A small seconds-showing drum *n* is set upon the seconds arbor of the movement.

> *Clocks combined with advertising apparatus.*
> Another drum of plates or cards presents advertisements.

Fitsch was granted a further patent in England on 7 May 1903 (no. 10,398), for a modified design which cured the problem relating to the hour plates turning over too soon.

The clocks were known as 'Ticket', 'Plato' or 'Chronos' clocks. The 'Plato' name thought to have come from the shape of the case, which was meant to resemble the lantern used by Plato when he searched for 'an honest man'. Later versions were sold in the 1930s, as 'Chronos' clocks. The first manufacturer of these clocks was the American Electrical and Novelty & Manufacturing Company of New York, where more than 40,000 were made. In the early part of the twentieth century, such clocks could be purchased from a number of English importers, particularly J.J. Elliott Ltd, who advertised 'Ever-Ready Chronos Clocks' in nickel or gold cases for thirty shillings (about £1.50) and with an alarm for 37s 6d (about £1.88).

While Fitsch tried to improve the action of the ticket release it remained a problem, and getting it to work efficiently without ever releasing two or more tickets at once was exacerbated as the clocks grew older. As a result, these clocks still send a cold shiver down the spine of any clock restorer asked to have a look at one.

Purchased in 1987
(Reg. 1987,10–12.62)

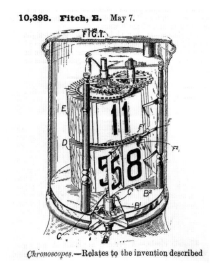

10,398. **Fitch, E.** May 7.

Chronoscopes.—Relates to the invention described

Jaeger Le Coultre

Atmos clock
Geneva, c.1950
Height 23.5 cm, width 21 cm, depth 16 cm

The idea of a so-called perpetual-motion clock probably first emerged in the form of a magnificent monumental clock, made for James Cox of London, which was powered by a mechanism that reacted to changes in barometric pressure. That clock is now in the Victoria & Albert Museum and is not in fact a perpetual motion machine because it draws its energy from changes in air pressure which wind a driving spring.

The 'Atmos' clock made by the well-known Swiss firm of Jaeger Le Coultre, has its origins in a design of clock introduced by Jean Léon Reutter in 1928. He gained a French patent for his design in November of that year and a Swiss one in March 1931. The clocks were originally manufactured in Paris by the Société de Radiologie in 1930, but by 1936 Jacques-David Le Coultre had seen one of Reutter's clocks and decided that the quality could be improved. The first new 'Atmos' clocks were made by Jaeger Le Coultre and were much superior to Reutter's earlier version, being powered by a sensitive gas-thermometer with ethyl-chloride contained in a metallic bellows which expanded and contracted with changes in temperature. In this ingenious mechanism, changes in the size of the bellows are transferred to create a winding action for the clock's mainspring. In this example the clock is designed to wind only as a result of a decrease in temperature and not when the temperature increases. Because the clock mechanism is similar in some ways to a typical four-hundred-day clock, very small movements can be used to keep the clock wound up all the time. It was claimed that a change of one degree Celsius would suffice to wind the clock enough to keep it going for one-hundred-and-twenty hours.

These new 'Atmos' clocks were immediately popular and remained so after the Second World War and into the 1950s. They are still being manufactured in much the same style today. This example is a standard version with a case glazed on all sides and with gold-plated base and panel frames. The movement is spring-driven, with a rotating torsion pendulum in the form of a large gilt-brass drum suspended from a long thin suspension spring made from elinvar. This metal alloy has a very low coefficient of linear expansion and is used here to reduce the effects on the length and elasticity of the spring, caused by temperature change.

An intriguing feature of this clock is that the maker's name does not appear anywhere; there is only the serial number 125425 on the front movement plate.

Bequeathed by Dr Eric Dingwall in 1986
(Reg. 1986,10–25.1)

Glossary

Armillary sphere

A representation of the heavens reduced to a series of metal bands with the earth at its centre. The most common bands are those for the horizon, the celestial equator, the tropics and the ecliptic, as well as a chosen number of meridians. There may also be pointers to show the positions of stars.

Aspectarium

A diagram designed to show the aspect or angular relationship between celestial bodies; particularly the sun, moon and earth. The most common aspects are opposition (180°) shown as an infinity sign, trine (120°) a triangle and quartile (90°) shown as a square.

Astrolabe

A sophisticated instrument consisting of a two-dimensional representation of the heavenly sphere, as seen from the geographical pole, projected onto a flat surface. It consists of a hollow plate or *mater* with a rim around the outside known as the *limb*. Contained in the mater is a plate or series of plates engraved with the projected lines for the equator, the tropics of Cancer and Capricorn as well as specific lines of celestial 'latitude' and 'longitude'. The plates are engraved specifically for use at set latitudes. Over the plate is a pierced *rete* with a representation of the constellations of the ecliptic and usually a number of star pointers with named stars. On the front, pivoted at the centre, is an index or *rule* and on the reverse, also pivoted at the centre, is an *alidade* or sight with two small vanes or plates at right angles to the alidade each with a pinnule or sighting hole used for taking observations and observing angles. The reverse of an astrolabe is usually engraved with calendrical information and often with a scale for ascertaining the time by observation as well as a shadow square which can be used for measuring angles. At the top of the instrument is a shackle and suspension ring. While the instrument proper is a hand-held device designed to be carried, it was also incorporated as an automatic indicator in sophisticated clocks, particularly of Germanic origin made in the sixteenth and seventeenth centuries.

Balance–dumb-bell

The equivalent in watches and small clocks to the foliot in medieval clocks. The dumb-bell consists of a small weighted bar which looks like a miniature dumb-bell and provides the timekeeping element in the watch. Like the foliot, the dumb-bell has no natural period of oscillation and so will swing faster or slower depending on the amount of impulse given to it by the escape wheel (see escapement). In the more sophisticated versions, the small disc-shaped weight at each end of the bar is adjustable to allow for fine regulation, although like the foliot controlled clock, accuracy of better than half an hour per day could not be expected.

Balance spring

A spiral spring used in portable timekeepers. When attached at one end to an oscillating balance wheel and at the other to the fixed plate of the watch or clock, it produces an isochronous timekeeper in which the balance takes the same time to swing through large or small arcs. This invention is credited to Robert Hooke (1635–1703) who commissioned a watch to be made by Thomas Tompion in 1675 and inscribed *Robert Hooke invent 1658. T. Tompion fecit 1675*. This was done in response to a claim by Christiaan Huygens for the invention. The new device improved the accuracy of portable timekeepers in the same way that the pendulum solved the problems of static machines and while its main application was in watches, it was nevertheless fundamental to the progress of marine timekeeping in the eighteenth century and beyond.

Balance – temperature compensated

The controlling device in a portable timekeeper which is designed to automatically compensate for the effects on the balance spring and balance caused by changes in temperature. The standard design in the nineteenth century, was based on an original by Thomas Earnshaw. It consists of a single cross arm to which are attached two bimetal strips, normally of brass and steel which are free to move at their open ends. In temperature change, the arms will move either inwards or outwards and will therefore move large weights on the arms which will change the radius of oscillation of the balance to counteract changes, particularly changes in the elasticity of the balance spring.

Balance wheel

The oscillating wheel in a clock or watch which controls the rate at which the device will run and consequently determines the accuracy of its time-keeping. Found in medieval clocks and watches before the introduction of the balance spring in 1675, the balance wheel, like the foliot and dumb-bell balance had no natural period of oscillation and consequently, its time-keeping ability was affected by changes in impulse given to keep it moving by the escape wheel. The balance wheel was superseded in 1657 by the introduction of the pendulum (see entry) for static clocks and by the application of a spiral balance spring (see entry) to the balance wheel for portable timekeepers by both Christiaan Huygens and Robert Hooke independently in 1675.

Calendar – Julian

Introduced by Julius Caesar in 45 BC to bring the length of the civil year closer to the true length of the mean tropical year of 365.2425 days. Months were either 30 or 31 days long except for February which was 29 days. Each year was 365 days long but a leap year of 366 days occurred every fourth year producing an average year of 365.25 days.

Calendar – Gregorian

A new calendar introduced by Pope Gregory XIII in 1582 which was intended to correct the error in the Julian calendar between the length of the civil year and the true tropical year. By that time it had accrued so that the year began ten days too early. The reform decreed that 4 October 1582 would be followed by 15 October to bring the calendar back into line with the true year. It also decreed that the year would be 365 days long with a leap year every fourth year except for years divisible by 100 although years divisible by 400 would be counted as ordinary years. Thus there are 97 leap years in every 400 year period and these adjustments produced a long-term accuracy for the new calendar which keeps the civil and tropical years in close harmony so that the accrued error is just one day in every 3300 years. It should be remembered, however, that the new Gregorian calendar was not universally adopted throughout Europe. The first countries to change were Italy, Spain, Portugal and Poland but it was not introduced in England until 1752 and in Russia it was not used until 1918.

Carillon clock

A clock which plays identifiable music on a series of bells at pre-determined intervals, in contrast to other musical clocks which produce their music on a miniature organ, or clocks which play simple chimes at the hours and quarters on a small number of bells. Thus, the great clock at Westminster Palace (Houses of Parliament) is a quarter chiming clock playing the simple progression of the Westminster chimes at the quarters but the Cathedral clock in Utrecht in The Netherlands is a carillon clock which plays a complete piece of music on the cathedral bells.

Cycloid

The path traced by a point on the circumference of a circle as the circle rolls along a straight line.

Dominical Letter

The Sunday letter derived from the first seven days in January which are each given a letter A-G and the letter allotted to the first Sunday is the letter for that year. Thus in 2003 the first Sunday is 5 January so the Dominical letter for 2003 is 'E'. In leap years the normal Dominical Letter is used until 28th February and thereafter the next letter is used so the year has two letters, in this case 'DC'. The next year, when the first Sunday in January falls on the 2nd the Dominical Letter will be 'B'. Knowledge of the Dominical letter for any year allows for the determination of the dates of Sundays for the whole year.

Epact

The age of the moon on the first day of the year – in England, before the introduction of the Gregorian calendar this was 25 March, the Vernal Equinox, when the sun in the zodiac passes through the first point of Aries. It is this factor which is used in the calculation of the date of Easter.

Escapement – anchor

An escapement used in clocks from about 1671. Although it is found primarily in longcase clocks, it can also be found in table, bracket and wall clocks although in this use it is far less commonly found.

Escapement – constant-force

An escapement in which impulse is given to the controlling device, a swinging pendulum or an oscillating balance, at every oscillation of the balance or swing of the pendulum. The escapement was developed by Thomas Mudge in his marine Timekeeper No. 1 but was also published in 1766 by Alexander Cumming in 'The Elements of Clock and Watch Work'.

Escapement – cross-beat

A clock escapement developed in south Germany and Prague by Jost Bürgi in about 1585 but first published in 1569 by Jacques Besson. The escapement is similar to the verge escapement, but here, the two pallets are mounted on separate arbors which are geared together by toothed sectors mounted on the arbors. At the end of each pallet arbor is a cross arm with weights. The length and weight of the two arms determine the rate at which the clock runs rather in the manner of a double foliot.

Escapement – dead-beat

Invented for precision clocks by George Graham in about 1715, the dead-beat escapement improved accuracy by having 'dead'-acting faces on the pallets. When the pendulum is swinging through its supplementary arc (when not locking or unlocking the escapement) the sliding action of the pallets on the escape wheel teeth cause no movement in the escape wheel thus reducing the interference which the clock has on the pendulum.

Escapement – gravity

A form of escapement developed towards the end of the eighteenth century in which the impulse to the pendulum is provided by gravity arms which are released by the pendulum and reset by the gear train so that all impulses are the same based on the weight of the gravity arm and the distance through which it falls while it is in contact with the pendulum. First introduced in England by Alexander Cumming and Thomas Mudge in about 1774/5.

Escapement – verge

The earliest common form of clock and watch escapement consists of two pallets mounted on a staff or verge, which interact with the teeth of the escape wheel (crown wheel). This crown wheel derives its power from the gear train connected to it and ultimately from the driving force produced either by a falling weight or a coiled spring. As the foliot or balance swings to and fro it causes the pallets or flags on the verge to alternately intercept and release the teeth of the crown wheel allowing it to turn only one tooth at a time and at the rate at which the foliot, balance or pendulum is swinging. It is this action which determines the rate of the clock. At the same time, the teeth of the crown wheel give a small push to the pallets on the verge to keep it moving and thus keep the foliot or balance swinging.

Foliot

A controlling device in the form of a horizontal bar with adjustable weights, found in medieval clockwork. The escape wheel in the clock causes the bar to oscillate back and forth and the bar's mass and length determine the rate at which it swings. Attached to the foliot is the verge staff with pallets which alternately lock and unlock the escape wheel, thus controlling the rate at which the wheels in the clock turn. Moving the adjustable weights inwards or outwards will make the foliot swing faster or slower, thus allowing adjustment to the rate at which the clock runs to achieve more accurate timekeeping. The foliot, however, has no natural period of swing inherent in its design and will go faster or slower depending on the amount of impulse given to it by the escape wheel. For this reason, clocks controlled by a foliot could never be accurate timekeepers and consequently early foliot controlled clocks were erratic in their time indication and could not be expected to achieve an accuracy of better than a quarter of an hour per day.

Frame – posted frame

In clocks the gear wheels and pinions are planted between bearing plates of which there are two main types. The earliest, which derives from turret clock construction, is the posted frame.

Frame – plated

By the end of the fifteenth century, but more commonly in the sixteenth century and onwards, the plated frame construction became the normal practice in which the various wheels etc were pivoted in bearing holes in two substantial flat plates separated by a series of pillars.

Fusee

A device invented some time during the fifteenth century which is used to even out the unequal force produced by a mainspring as it unwinds. A spiral groove is cut on a changing profile cone-like component. A line or chain is wound around the spring barrel. When the fusee is turned to wind the clock, the line is pulled off the barrel on to the fusee, turning the barrel and winding the spring. When the spring is fully wound, the line pulls on the smalllest diameter of the fusee. The fusee turns the gear train and as the clock runs, the spring pulls the line off the fusee and back on to the barrel until at the end of the run the line is pulling on the largest diameter of the fusee, thus giving it a mechanical advantage and adding to the effect power of the weaker pull of the spring.

Gimbals

A device used for mounting marine chronometers on board ships. It consists of four pivots arranged in groups of two so that the chronometer carried in the gimbals will always remain horizontal irrespective of the motion of the ship.

Going barrel

A mainspring barrel in a clock or watch in which the great wheel is mounted on the barrel itself and the mainspring produces torque in the direction of motion of the going train. A ratchet system prevents the mainspring from unwinding in the wrong direction.

Going train

The wheels and pinions in a clock or watch which transmit motion from the driving force, usually a weight or spring, to the escapement. In an eight-day clock and most watches these usually consist of four wheels and three pinions: great wheel, centre wheel (which rotates once per hour and carries the minute hand), third wheel and fourth wheel (in watches arranged to rotate once per minute to carry a seconds hand).

Golden number

A year number based on the cyclic relationship between the sun and moon based on a period of 19 years. The ancient Greek Meton discovered the 19-year relationship – 19 years are equal to 6,939.75 days and 235 lunations are equal to 6,939.689 days, a difference of only 2 hours. The year number 1–19 was used to arrange religious festivals, dependent on the phase of the moon. It takes 19 years for a new moon to fall on the same date with the same week-day. The name derives from the fact that the ancient Greeks are said to have had dates written in gold on public monuments.

Hours – Babylonian hours

A system used by the ancient Babylonians in which the day of twenty-four equal hours began at sunrise.

Hours – Italian or Bohemian

A system of counting the hours used in Medieval Bohemia and Poland and some parts of Germany in which the day began at sunset and was divided into twenty-four equal hours.

Hours – Nuremberg

In medieval Nuremberg, from sunset onwards, the night hours were numbered 1 onwards until sunrise and then the day hours were counted until sunset. Thus at the vernal and autumnal equinoxes there would be twelve day and twelve night hours but at the summer solstice there would be sixteen day hours and eight night hours and at the winter solstice there would be eight day hours and sixteen night hours. In order to keep pace with the changing seasons, the reckoning would have to be changed every three weeks so that the day and night hour periods would reflect the actual periods of daylight and darkness. The system was abandoned in 1489.

Hours – unequal, seasonal or temporal
A system in which the hours of daylight and the hours of darkness are each divided into 12 equal parts. In this method of reckoning, in winter the dark hours are long and the light hours short while in summer the opposite is true. On the equinoxes all hours would be equal and at the solstices they would differ most. A similar system was used in Japanese clocks until the end of the Edo period in 1873.

Lunar month (lunation)
The interval between two successive appearances of the new moon – normally 29.53 mean solar days although it can vary by as much as thirteen hours.

Maintaining power
A mechanism incorporated in a clock designed to keep it running whilst it is being wound up. Both spring and weight-driven clocks have a tendency to either stop or even run backwards when they are being wound. For this reason various methods were devised to provide power to the escapement while winding was taking place. The earliest form was developed by Christiaan Huygens in his designs for the first pendulum clocks of the 1660s. Here an endless cord and a pulley system for the driving weight ensured that the weight was always pulling on the driving sprocket even when the cord was being pulled to wind the clock.

The next system was bolt-and-shutter maintaining power. A lever was pulled which moved shutters that covered the winding squares and at the same time cocked a spring-loaded bolt. This engaged in one of the gear wheels to provide power whilst the driving weights were being raised during winding.

In the eighteenth century, John Harrison devised a spring loaded mechanism for use in his marine timekeepers. In this device a spring powered ratchet situated in the great-wheel and fusee assembly exerted force on the great wheel when the machine was being wound. This system was adopted for more sophisticated portable clocks such as marine chronometers and also was extensively used in watches in the nineteenth century.

Marquetry
A form of decoration in furniture and clock cases in which patterns are formed by the inlaying of different woods and/or other materials into a wooden background. In clock cases, the most common form was floral marquetry during the third quarter of the seventeenth century in which intricate designs of birds and flowers were made up by inlaying a walnut base veneer with stained woods and ivory to produce a stunning effect.

Nef
A table ornament in the form of a medieval ship. The word probably derives from the old French word for a form of ship. These table ornaments have their origins as early as the twelfth century and were simple boats intended to carry such things as salt, spices, napkins or drinking vessels etc. By the sixteenth century the table nef had become elaborate in form with masts and rigging and perhaps the most sophisticated of all nefs were the automated versions made by Hans Schlottheim in Augsburg.

Rise-and-fall regulation
A system devised for use in larger table clocks to enable the rate of the clock to be adjusted from the front of the clock without having to turn the clock around to gain access to the pendulum from the back. The mechanism normally consists of a subsidiary dial and hand on the

main dial. Turning the hand turns a cam on the back of the dial which in turn raises or lowers a lever mechanism on the back of the clock. The pendulum suspension is fitted to the end of the lever and the suspension spring passes between two blocks. Turning the hand raises or lowers the pendulum and consequently alters the effective length of the pendulum, thereby changing its rate.

Stop-work
In spring-driven clocks with fusee, there is a rachet system called set-up, used to prevent the mainspring from fully running down. The stop-work consists of a block mounted on the clock plate in which is pivoted the stop iron. When the winding is nearly complete and the line or chain is nearly all on the fusee, the line or chain will move the stop iron into the path of a hook on the end of the fusee to prevent further winding. When the clock runs the line or chain is pulled off the rotating fusee back onto the mainspring barrel until all the line is all off the fusee and is taut, thus preventing any further rotation of the fusee. In this way, the clockmaker can determine which part of the mainspring is used. This is normally in the area of the middle turns where the torque output is at its most constant.

Striking mechanism – count-wheel
The earliest form of striking mechanism in which the number of blows struck on the bell is controlled by a wheel around which slots are cut at increasing distances. This count-wheel rotates once in twelve hours or once in twenty-four hours depending on the system and allows the striking train to run progressively longer each time the striking train is released to strike the hours 1–12 or 1–24.

Striking mechanism – Grande-sonnerie
A sophisticated system of striking in which the quarter and the full hour are struck at each quarter-hour.

Striking mechanism – Rack
A system of striking invented in about 1670 by the Reverend Edward Barlow in which the number of blows struck on the bell is controlled by a rack whose movement is itself controlled by a stepped, snailed cam mounted on the hour wheel which rotates once in twelve hours.

Temperature compensation devices
By the end of the seventeenth century clocks had achieved sufficient accuracy in their performance that variations in timekeeping caused by changes in temperature were recognised as a problem which needed to be overcome. During the eighteenth century various methods of providing compensation were devised.

The first was the mercurial pendulum invented by George Graham in 1721: a bottom-supported jar contains mercury which expands up or down to compensate for changes in the length of the pendulum rod as it expands in heat or shrinks in cold.

In 1725 John Harrison was investigating the expansion of metals caused by the effects of heat and cold, an investigation which resulted in his gridiron pendulum of 1727–1728. It consisted of five steel rods, including the pendulum rod itself, and four brass rods arranged in a frame which allowed them to move freely in relation to the pendulum rod and rivetted so that the steel rods expand downwards and the brass rods expand upwards in such a way that the pendulum bob maintains a constant position in changing temperatures.

By the middle of the third quarter of the eighteenth century portable timekeepers had also achieved such accuracy that they needed some form of temperature compensation. It was not until 1765, however, that Pierre Le Roy in Paris invented the first self-compensating balance in which an attached mechanism fitted to the oscillating balance changed its shape to compensate for changes in the elasticity of the balance spring caused by changes is temperature. Before this, temperature compensation in watches and chronometers took the form of applied bimetal strips which reacted to temperature change and acted on the balance spring changing its effective length to make it operate faster or slower.

In more recent times, pendulum rods for accurate regulators have been made from a metal alloy called Invar. This alloy has the property that it only changes in length by tiny amounts or, in some cases, not at all, when the temperature changes.

Time – equation of time The difference between true solar time shown by a sundial or solar observation and mean solar time measured by a clock. The difference between the two results from the fact that a clock shows time at a constant rate whereas the apparent motion of the sun through the heavens is not constant. The fact that the Earth's orbit around the sun is elliptical and also that the Earth's axis is tilted to the celestial equator by 23.5 degrees produces this variation. There are four days in the year when both clock and sundial agree, on about 15 April, 13 June, 2 September and 25 December. The maximum positive occurs on about 12 February when the clock is almost 14.5 minutes ahead of the sun and the minimum occurs on about 3 November when the clock is almost 16.5 minutes behind the sun.

Time – mean solar day
Twenty-four equal hours measured by a clock.

Time – sidereal day
The period between two successive transits of a fixed star equal to 23 hours 56 minutes 4.1 seconds of mean solar time.

Time – true solar day
The period between two successive transits of the sun, a period which varies throughout the year (see equation of time).

Tourbillon
A device patented by Abraham Louis Breguet of Paris in 1801 and later used by other watch makers in high quality carriage clocks, pocket watches and pocket chronometers. It consists of a constantly revolving carriage on which the escapement and balance are mounted. By continuously changing their position, vertical positional errors, caused by changes in the attitude of the watch when it is being carried, are nullified.

Up-and-down indicator
A dial found on spring-driven machines, most commonly marine and pocket chronometers, which showed the state of wind of the mainspring. These dials were sometimes fitted to marine chronometers where allowing the chronometer to run down and stop could have catastrophic results.

Further Reading and Reference

Abeler, Jurgen, *Meister der Uhrmacherkunst*, Wuppertal, 1977

Allix & Bonnert, *Carriage Clocks*, Antique Collectors' Club, Woodbridge, 1974

Andrewes, et al., *The Quest for Longitude*, Harvard University, 1996

Antiquarian Horology, Journal of the Antiquarian Horological Society, 1953 onwards

Atkins & Overall, *Some Account of the Worshipful Company of Clockmakers*, London, 1881

Augarde, Jean-Dominique, *Les Ouvres du Temps*, Antiquorum Geneva, 1996

Baillie, G.H., *Clocks and Watches, An Historic Bibliography*, NAG Press 1951, reprint 1978

Baillie, Clutton & Ilbert, *Britten's Old Clocks & Watches and their Makers*, 9th ed. Methuen, London, 1982

Barder, R., *The Georgian Bracket Clock*, Antique Collectors' Club, Woodbridge, 1993

Barder, Richard, *English Country Grandfather Clocks*, David & Charles, Newton Abbot, 1983

Bassermann-Jordan, Ernst von, *The Book of Old Clocks and Watches*, Allen and Unwin, London, 1964

Beeson, C.F.C., *English Church Clocks*, Brant Wright Associates, 1977

Bird, Anthony, *English House Clocks 1650–1850*, David & Charles, Devon, 1973

Bobinger, Maximilian, *Kunstuhrmacher in Alt-Augsburg*, Augsburg, 1969

Breguet, Emmanuel *Breguet, Watchmakers since 1775*, Alain de Gourcoff, Paris, 1997

Brusa, Giuseppe, *L'Arte Dell' Orologeria in Europa*, Bramante, Milan, 1978

Bruton, Eric, *The History of Clocks and Watches*, Orbis, London, 1979

Bruton, Eric, *The Longcase Clock*, Granada, Hertfordshire, 1977

Cescinsky & Webster, *English Domestic Clocks*, 2nd Edition, Routledge [n.d.]

Cipolla, C.M., *Clocks & Culture 1300–1700*, Collins, London, 1967

Collard, F.B. Royer, *Skeleton Clocks*, NAG Press, London, 1969

Coole, P.G. & Neumann E., *The Orpheus Clocks*, Hutchinson, London, 1972

Cumhail, P.W., *Investing in Clocks and Watches*, Barrie & Rockliffe, London, 1967

Daniels, George, *The Art of Breguet*, Sotheby, London, 1974

Darken & Hooper, *English 30-Hour Clocks*, Penita Books, Woking, 1997

Dawson, Drover, Parkes, *Early English Clocks*, Antique Collectors Club, Woodbridge, 1982

De Carle, Donald, *Watch & Clock Encyclopedia*, NAG Press, London, 1975

Dohrn-Van Rossum, *History of the Hour*, English translation, University of Chicago Press, 1996

Earnshaw, Thomas, *An Appeal to the Public*, London, 1808

Edwardes, Ernest, L, *The Story of the Pendulum Clock*, Sherratt & Son, Altringham, 1977

Edwardes, Ernest, L. *The Grandfather Clock*, Sherratt & Son, Altringham, 1971

Edwards, Ernest, *Weight-driven Chamber Clocks of the Middle Ages and Renaissance*, Sherratt, Altringham, 1965

Ewing Duncan, David, *The Calendar*, Fourth Estate, 1998

Fritsch, Julia, et al., *Ships of Curiosity, Three Renaissance Automata*, Réunion, Paris, 2001

Gazeley, W.J, *Clock and Watch Escapements*, Butterworth, Kent, 1973

Good, Richard, *Victorian Clocks*, British Museum Press, London 1996

Good, Richard, *Britten's Handbook Dictionary and Guide*, Bloomsbury Books, London, 1982

Gould, Rupert, *The Marine Chronometer Its history and Development*, Holland Press, London, 1923, reprinted Antique Collectors' Club, Woodbridge, 1990

Gordon, G.F.C., *Clockmaking Past and Present*, Oxford, 1949

Grimthorpe, Lord, *Clocks Watches & Bells*, Crosby, Lockwood & Son, London, 1903

Harrison, John, *Principles and Explanations of Timekeepers by Harrison, Arnold and Earnshaw*, 1767, British Horological Institute, facsimile with introduction by J. Betts, 1984

Haswell, Eric, *Horology, The Science of Time Measurement*, Charles River Books, Boston, Mass., 1976

Hawkins, J.B., *Thomas Cole and Victorian Clockmaking*, Macarthur Press, Sydney, 1975

Heuer & Maurice, *European Pendulum Clocks*, Schiffer Publishing, Atglen, 1988

Horological Journal, Journal of the British Horological Institute

Horological Masterworks, Antiquarian Horological Society, Ticehurst, 2003

Howse, Derek *Greenwich Time*, Oxford University Press, 1980

Huygens, Christiaan, *Oeuvres Completès de Christiaan Huygens*, The Hague, 1931

Huygens, Christiaan, *Horologium 1658*, with English translation by E.L. Edwardes, *Antiquarian Horology*, Vol. VII, pp. 35–55

Jagger, Cedric, *The World's Great Clocks and Watches*

Jagger, Cedric, *Royal Clocks*, Robert Hale, London

Kaltenböck, Frederick *Vienna Timepieces*, Günther, 1993

King, Henry, C., *Geared to the Stars*, Adam Hilger, Bristol 1978

Landes, David, *Revolution in Time: Clocks and the making of the modern world*, Harvard University, 1983

Laycock, W.S., *The Lost Science of John 'Longitude' Harrison*, Brant Wright Assoc. Ashford, 1976

Lee, *The Knibb Family*, Ernest Benn Ltd, Byfleet, 1964

Leopold, J.H. *The Almanus Manuscript*, Hutchinson, London, 1971

Lippincott et al, *The Story of Time*, National Maritime Museum exhibition catalogue, Merrell Holberton, 2000

Lloyd, H. Alan, *Chats on Old Clocks*, Country Life, 1964

Lloyd, H. Alan, *Some Outstanding Clocks Over 700 Years*, Leonard Hill, London, 1958

Lloyd, H. Alan, *The Collector's Dictionary of Clocks*, New York, 1964

Loomes, Brian, *Country Clocks and their London Origins*, David & Charles, 1976

Loomes, Brian, *Grandfather Clocks and their Cases*, Bracken Books, London, 1985

Loomes, Brian, *Painted Dial Clocks*, Antique Collectors' Club, Woodbridge, 1994

Loomes, Brian, *Watchmakers and Clock Makers of the World*, vol. 2, London, 1976

Loomes, Brian, *Early Clockmakers of Great Britain*, NAG Press, London, 1981

Maurice, Klaus & Otto, Hans, *The Clockwork Universe*, Neale Watson Academic Publications, New York, 1980

Maurice, Klaus, *Die Deutsche Räderuhr*, 2 vols. C.H. Beck, Munich, 1976

Mercer, Vaudrey *Arnold and Son*, Antiquarian Horological Society, 1972

Mercer, Vaudrey, *Edward John Dent*, Antiquarian Horological Society, 1977

Mercer, Vaudrey, *The Frodshams*, Antiquarian Horological Society, 1981

Mody, N.H.N., *Japanese Clocks*, Routledge Kegan & Paul, London, reprint 1968

Mudge, Thomas junior, *A Description with Plates*, facsimile reprint, 1799 edition, London, 1977

Needham, Joseph, *Heavenly Clockwork*, Cambridge University Press, 1960

Nicholls, A., *Clocks in Colour*, Blandford Press, Dorset, 1975

North, J.D., *Richard of Wallingford*, 3 vols, Oxford University Press, 1976

Ord-Hulme, A.W.G. *The Musical Clock*, Mayfield Books, Ashborne, 1995

Palmer, Brooks, *Treasury of American Clocks*, Macmillan, New York, 1967

Pioneers of Precision Timekeeping, Monograph No. 3, Antiquarian Horological Society [n.d.]

Plomp, R., *Spring-Driven Dutch Pendulum Clocks*, Interbook International, Schiedam, 1979

Quill, H., *The Man Who Found Longitude*, John Baker, London, 1966

Randall, Anthony, G. *The Time Museum Catalogue of Chronometers*, Rockford, 1992

Rawlins, A.L., *The Science of Clocks and Watches*, Pitman, New York, 1948

Reese, Abraham, *Clocks Watches and Chronometers 1819–1820*, reprint, David & Charles, 1970

Reid, *Treatise on Clock and Watch Making Theoretical and Practical*, 1855

Roberts, Derek, *British Longcase Clocks*, Schiffer, West Chester, 1990

Roberts, Derek, *British Skeleton Clocks*, Antique Collectors' Club, Woodbridge, 1987

Roberts, Derek, *Carriage and Other Travelling Clocks*, Schiffer Publishing, Atglen, 1993

Roberts, Derek, *Mystery, Novelty & Fantasy Clocks*, Schiffer Publishing, Atglen, Pennsylvania, 1999

Roberts, Derek, *Precision Pendulum Clocks*, Schiffer Publishing Ltd, Atglen, 2003

Roberts, Derek, English Precision Pendulum Clocks, Schiffer Publishing Ltd, Atglen, 2003

Roberts, Deryk, *The Bracket Clock*, David & Charles, Newton Abbot, 1982

Robertson, J. Drummond, *The Evolution of Clockwork*, E.P. Group, Yorks. 1972

Robey, John, *The Longcase Clock Reference Book*, 2 vols, Mayfield Books, Mayfield, 2001

Robinson, Tom, *The Longcase Clock*, Antique Collectors' Club, 1981

Robinson, T.R. *Modern Clocks*, NAG Press, London, 1955

Rose, Ronald, *English Dial Clocks*, Antique Collectors' Club, Woodbridge, 1978.

Royer Collard, F.B., *Skeleton Clocks*, NAG Press, London, 1969

Sellink, J.L., *Dutch Antique Domestic Clocks*, H.E. Sternfert Kroese, Leiden, 1973

Shenton, Rita, *Christopher Pinchbeck and his Family*, Brant Wright Associates, Ashford, 1976.

Shenton, Alan & Rita, *The Price Guide to Collectable Clocks*, Antique Collectors' Club, Woodbridge, 1985

Smith, A., (ed.) *Dictionary of Clocks*, London, 1979

Symonds, R.W., *Thomas Tompion, His Life and Works*, Batsford, 1951

Tait, Hugh, *Clocks And Watches*, British Museum Press, London, 1983

Tardy, *French Clocks* vol. I, II, III, Tardy, Paris [n.d.]

Tardy, *Dictionnaire des Horlogers Français*, Paris, 1972

Tennant, Margaret, *Longcase Painted Dials*, N.A.G. Press, London, 1995

Tyler, E.J. *Black Forest Clocks*, NAG Press, London, 1977

Ullyet, Kenneth, *Clocks and Watches*, Paul Hamlyn, London, 1971

Ullyet, Kenneth, *In Quest of Clocks and Watches*, Spring Books, London, 1969

White, George, *English Lantern Clocks*, Antique Collector's Club, Woodbridge, 1989

Wood, E.J. *Curiosities of Clocks*, London, 1866

Photographic Acknowledgements

All photographs © The Trustees of
The British Museum, unless otherwise
stated.

p. 82
English School, *c.*1680, Royal
Observatory from Crooms Hill
© National Maritime Museum.

p. 102
Portrait of George Graham by Thomas
Hudson, *c.*1745
© The Science Museum.

p. 108
© The Antiquarian Horological Society.

p. 112
Reproduced by kind permission of
Charles Frodsham & Co Ltd.

p. 116
Observatory tent from W. Wales and
W. Bayly, *The Original Astronomical
Observatory made in the years 1772, 1773,
1774 and 1775*. London, 1777.

p. 130
John Arnold & Son watch-paper,
Department of Prints and Drawings,
British Museum, Banks 39.6.

p. 132
Portrait of Thomas Earnshaw by Sir
Martin Archer Shee, 1798.
© The Science Museum.

p. 146
Tradecard of John Dwerrihouse
Department of Prints and Drawings,
British Museum, Banks 39.43

p. 148
Portrait of Sir William Congreve, Royal
Artillery Institution.

p. 150 Premises of 14 Cornhill taken
from *London Street Views* by John Tallis,
c. 1844. Guildhall Library, Corporation
of London.

p. 154
Portrait of Chauncey Jerome,
© The Conneticut Historical Society,
Hartford, Conneticut.

p. 160
Premises of 14 Soho Square taken from
London Street Views by John Tallis, *c.*
1838, Guildhall Library, Corporation of
London.

p. 162
Patent, The Public Record Office, Kew,
Surrey.

Index

Photographic Acknowledgements

Index